D1681454

Southern Tier MEMORIES

VOLUME II ~ THE '40s, '50s & '60s

presented by

Press & Sun-Bulletin
pressconnects.com

ACKNOWLEDGEMENTS

For most residents of Greater Binghamton, the 1940s, '50s and '60s shaped the way we live today. We dedicate this book to the people who helped develop the area – many of whom grew up here and still live here today.

The men and women of the Broome County Historical Society made this book possible. It is through their vision, keen instinct and hard work that we have these images that reflect life in those exciting days. We thank them for their efforts.

We would also like to thank the Newsroom and Market Development departments of the *Press & Sun-Bulletin* for their contribution to *Southern Tier Memories, Volume II – The 1940s, '50s and '60s: Images from the Broome County Historical Society*.

We are pleased to present our second family album, one we think captures the vigor and spirit of the people who made the Southern Tier a great place to live.

Bernie Griffin

Bernie Griffin
President and Publisher
Press & Sun-Bulletin

Copyright© 2002 • ISBN: 1-932129-12-X
All rights reserved. No part of this book may be reproduced, stored in a retrieval system or transmitted in any form or by any means, electronic, mechanical, photocopying, recording or otherwise, without prior written permission of the copyright owner or the publisher.
Published by Pediment Publishing, a division of The Pediment Group, Inc. www.pediment.com Printed in Canada

Table of Contents

Foreword 4

A Bird's Eye View 5

Street Scenes 13

Education 19

Commerce 35

Industry 61

Military 73

Public Service 81

Transportation 103

Society 115

Disasters 135

Recreation 143

Celebration 155

Foreword

Once the men and women of the Southern Tier did their part to defeat Hitler and Tojo, they began raising families. To do that they needed more schools, more churches, more places to shop, more automobiles, more factories and, in short, more of everything.

In 1940, the population of Broome County was 165,749. By 1970, it was 212,815, an increase of 28 percent. This book captures those years of explosive growth. Like *Volume I,* this book is a family album, one that shows our families exulting in the birth of children and lamenting the passing of loved ones.

Almost all of the photos in this book come from the archives of the Broome County Historical Society, many of them donated by the *Press & Sun-Bulletin.* The general public submitted some of the photos, and we are grateful for those contributions.

There are powerful photos in this book, ones that will make you smile as you share the joy of those captured on film. Others bring forth tears, such as the one that shows a young man days before he was killed in World War II, or the one that captures an almost unbelievable family tragedy during the Vietnam War.

The photos in this book capture the rich detail of life in the Southern Tier. The photos document the rise of the suburbs and the momentous change in the way we worked. Traditional, low-skill factory jobs began to be replaced by jobs that required more education and better training.

Sifting through the 20,000 photos of the society's collection, we were struck by the complexity of life, even during those simpler days of the 1940s, '50s and '60s. We think this book will give you an idea of what life was like during those days.

A Bird's Eye View

The best way to capture the natural beauty of the Southern Tier is to fly over it. Gentle valleys, meandering rivers and streams, and low hilltops provide pleasant scenes to contemplate.

An airplane ride through time, as these images attest, would reveal how communities change. Some prosper; others wither.

During the 1940s, '50s and '60s, vital new communities sprouted from once-empty fields in Vestal, Endwell, Conklin and Kirkwood. Better roads and automobiles helped fuel this growth, clearly visible from the air.

The new suburbs came at a price, one that was paid by Binghamton. In 1950 the city was home to 80,674 people, the most ever recorded by the U.S. Census Bureau. By 1960, there were 5,000 fewer people.

Even photos of the urban area tell this story. In Binghamton, the photo of the newly completed North Shore Drive shows a city cut off from the Susquehanna by a roadway that would soon be speeding people away.

By the mid-1950s, rows of shiny new houses were lining the new streets of Endwell, providing homes to the technicians and engineers who stoked the engines of IBM.

Empty land in the western Broome communities of Vestal and Union provided ample room for new houses, factories and schools. Developed land in Binghamton and Johnson City would soon be cleared for major new roadways that would help people get to the new, growing sections of the county.

View of Binghamton from the Ansco Film Plant looking east, 1941.

A BIRD'S EYE VIEW

View of Binghamton from the Ansco Film Plant looking north, 1941.

Aerial view of Vestal, September 1947.

Aerial view of Johnson City, 1953.

Aerial view of the north side of Binghamton, October 1953.

SOUTHERN TIER MEMORIES: VOLUME II

Aerial view of Johnson City looking northeast, September 1954.

A BIRD'S EYE VIEW

Aerial view of the traffic circle in Johnson City, October 1954.

Aerial view of Endicott, April 1955, at the intersection of Nanticoke Avenue and Main Street.

Aerial view of Endwell, 1957.

Aerial view of Endicott looking north along Washington Avenue toward North Street, August 1959.

8

Aerial view of Endicott with IBM factories.

A BIRD'S EYE VIEW

Aerial view of Nimmonsburg, in the Town of Chenango, March 1962. The Nimmonsburg School is in the center.

Aerial view of Vestal looking north, September 4, 1964.

A view of the Vestal Parkway and Ridgehaven Drive, October 1965.

Aerial view of Conklin, August 1965.

Aerial view of Windsor, circa 1966.

Town of Union at Choconut Center, September 1967.

A BIRD'S EYE VIEW

Aerial view of Binghamton after North Shore Drive was completed, April 1968.

STREET SCENES

In the 1950s, buildings erected in the early part of the century dominated the streets of Binghamton. On Chenango Street, the most easily recognized landmark remained the Press Building, which was the tallest building in the city.

Despite the city's age, shop owners and residents kept the main thoroughfares neat and tidy as the streets filled with automobiles. In the 1950s, in Binghamton as across the nation, city planners began searching for ways to re-energize the urban areas.

Soon, run-down residential areas such as Kenwood Avenue and old landmarks such as The Hotel Arlington would give way to newer buildings. The Kenwood Avenue area became home to the Government Plaza, which now houses the City Hall and county and state office buildings. The state building is now the tallest in the city.

Pictures of the urban landscape document the change national economic trends have brought to the Binghamton region. Montgomery Ward was once one of the leading department stores in downtown. By the 1970s, it had fled to a suburban shopping mall in Johnson City.

The Ward building is now home to the Broome County Department of Social Services, one of the first examples of government consolidation in the region. Binghamton, Union and other local governments had to run their own welfare departments until the county took on the responsibility.

Chenango Street, Binghamton, 1951.

STREET SCENES

Court Street, Binghamton, looking east, December 1947.

Binghamton Refrigeration Company at 287 Water Street, 1947.

Washington Avenue, Endicott, circa 1941.

Court and Chenango streets, Binghamton, 1952.

STREET SCENES

Main Street, Binghamton, 1951.

Kenwood Avenue, Binghamton, 1948. The street no longer exists. Government Plaza replaced the neighborhood.

16

Court and Chenango streets, Binghamton, October 1947.

Chenango at Henry Street, 1966.

Looking south on Chenango Street, Binghamton, 1950s.

STREET SCENES

Court and Chenango streets, Binghamton, 1963.

Winter scene on Court Street in Binghamton, December 1966.

Henry Street, looking west, Binghamton, circa 1969.

18

EDUCATION

In the 1940s, '50s and '60s, the main business of the region was education. New schools sprang up all across the valleys of the Susquehanna and Chenango. Older school districts constructed new buildings or renovated and expanded the old.

The Baby Boom generation was stamping its first footprint on the land. The burgeoning numbers of students required new classrooms and more teachers. Little could stand in the way, even 150-foot-tall elm trees.

The images from this era capture the end of long traditions. Boys and girls made sure they had on their best clothes before they would pose for a photographer. For boys that meant clean, white, and probably starched shirts. Formal suits and ties were the norm.

For girls, skirts and dresses provided plenty of fabric to comply with society's ideas about modesty.

There was little emphasis on breaking out of gender roles. Boys still dominated the public speaking classes, held the top jobs in student government and went to shop classes. Girls held support roles and filled out cheerleading squads.

For the region, one event with tremendous impact was the birth of Harpur College, now Binghamton University. The school was founded as an offshoot of Syracuse University and was known as Triple Cities College. Soon, it was bursting at the seams, and with the help of state Senator Warren M. Anderson, R-Binghamton, it became part of the new State University of New York.

Hillcrest pupils on their way to school walk across tracks at Nowlan Road (as a bus brings their schoolmates who live far enough to warrant rides), September 1959. The walk-or-ride controversy bedeviled the Chenango Valley district. The pupils are Sharon Worden, 6; brother Gary Worden, 11; Kenneth Graham, 8; and Lynne Secor, 8.

EDUCATION

East Junior High School boys class, 1944. *Courtesy Mary O'Dea-Murphy*

East Junior High School girls class, 1944. *Courtesy Mary O'Dea-Murphy*

Students from the Antone Beauty School on Chenango Street, Binghamton, 1947.

Town of Maine graduating class, 1948.

New officers of Endicott's George Washington School's PTA go over committee assignments, May 1951. Seated: First Vice-President Mrs. Paul Morrow, President Mrs. Richard Tompkins, Second Vice-President Mrs. Glenn Daniels. Standing: Recording Secretary Mrs. Charles H. Cheney and Treasurer Mrs. Daniel Pierce.

A 150-foot elm tree was knocked down to make room for the new Binghamton Central athletic field, 1953. Taxpayers spent $1,100,000 for the new gymnasium and football field.

EDUCATION

Graduates from the Antone Beauty School on Chenango Street, Binghamton, June 1948.

Students at a public speaking class hold guns used as props, March 1952. The students are Stephen Kubica, Douglas Underwood, Joseph Taylor and John Bohush.

Representatives from the classes at Horace Mann School give roses and mementos to Miss Maud H. Luscomb, principal for 14 years, February 1958. Front row, Heather Clark, Thomas Naylor, Gary Schanz and Michael Supa. Second row: Donna Springer, Neil Sivers, Vito Mastroiovanni, Miss Luscomb, John Guley, Dale Kennan, Patricia Doyle and Joy Supa. Rear: Kathleen Easton, Alyn Kenien, JohnMorreall, Paul Scolaro, Katherine Burnett and Peter Thornton.

EDUCATION

New officers of the Port Dickinson Junior High student organization, October 1953. Assistant Treasurer Donald MacDuffee, Treasurer Robert Young, Vice President Leonard Christian, President Gary Sullivan and Secretary Joyce Anderson.

Members of a woodshop class at Union-Endicott High School work on a shipping crate used to send supplies prepared by a homemaking class to the needy in Korea, November 1952. Pictured are Robert Kucera, Roger Rizzi, Gary Webb and Dale Berry.

Aerial view of Harpur College, May 1958.

The North High Majorettes work on their routine, October 1963.

EDUCATION

A skeleton provides Union-Endicott students with first-hand information about the human body and how it operates, May 1961. Biology Instructor Charles Turver explains movements of the arm bones to Joseph Nejeschleba and Bernadette Tovornik.

Drive Chairman Edgar S. Mulhollen stands in front of bundles of clothing collected by Union-Endicott pupils for shipment to needy children in the southern United States, December 1960. Pupils collected 192 bags of clothing during the Save the Children Federation Bundle Days Drive.

The Johnson City Marching Girls make an appearance in front of the Broome County Courthouse, circa 1963.

Aftermath from the old Chester B. Lord mansion demolition at 67 Riverside Drive. The wreckers are clearing the site for the construction of a school for physically handicapped children, September 1961.

EDUCATION

Workmen erect framework for the new gymnasium-auditorium at St. Ambrose's Parochial School at Broad Street and Garfield Avenue, Endicott.

Lloyd G. Scoville, vice-president of Miller Motors, hands car keys over to Harold Hess, director of driver training for the Binghamton high schools. Miller provided six cars at no cost to area high schools for driver education, December 1964.

Mrs. Wanda Kolpakas, instructor, at right, shows craft items to Mrs. Betty Reynolds, summer playground instructor, at a one-day institute held for school center instructors, Binghamton, July 1965.

Mrs. Clarice Knapp, right foreground, director of the Binghamton School of Practical Nursing, fastens a bright new white cap to the head of Miss Christine Tracy of Lisle, one of 24 graduates at the one-year school for licensed practical nurses, June 1965.

Mrs. Clarice Knapp, right, director of Binghamton School of Practical Nursing, "pins" Mrs. Fred Gaube as classmates look on during graduation ceremonies at Christopher Columbus School, February 1965.

Members of the Catholic Central High School yearbook staff, left to right: Maryann Muscato, Rose Cullen, Elizabeth Barron, editor, Susan Barth and Robert Save, co-editor, Binghamton, 1965.

Aerial view of SUNY-Binghamton, May 1966.

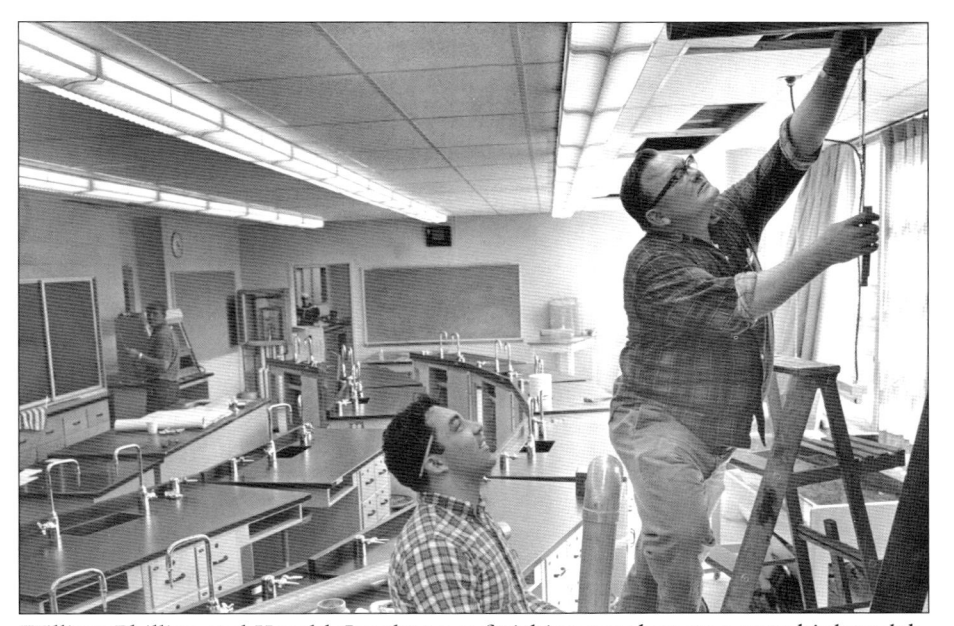

William Phillips and Harold Crocker put finishing touches on a new biology lab, circa 1968. The lab and equipment were paid for with a $320,463 bond issue.

EDUCATION

Sister M. Jovita, right, from the faculty of SS Cyril and Methodius Parochial School, teaches Sister Mary Magdalene, another teacher, how to change a tire, Binghamton, June 1965.

30

Guy Manning, of the Town of Conklin Highway Department, escorts students across Route 7 to the Susquehanna Valley elementary and junior-senior high school, September 1966. Manning worked as a temporary guard as the town was seeking a permanent guard following the death of a 15-year-old who was struck and killed by a truck.

EDUCATION

Members hold BCC's Circle "K" Club banner in preparation for the club's annual student talent show to benefit United Fund, October 1966. Students, from left: Andrea Piza, Brenda Wike, Sally Opka and Vicky Cole.

Sorting out names of 61 companies that are visiting the Broome Tech campus to hire seniors are Lawrence J. Sitterlee, director of the college's placement bureau and Mrs. Nan Newman, coordinator of the bureau, March 1966.

Student Council members of SS Cyril and Methodius School, 146 Clinton Street, Binghamton, November 1966. The Stars and Stripes once floated over the Capitol in Washington, a gift from Representative Howard W. Robison to the school. From left: Sister Joan, Michael Mulligan, Joanne Balan, Jeanne Lesko and Roseann Drobot.

Sister St. Cornelius and her eighth grade class go through a lesson (unrehearsed) as a mobile television recording crew from Marywood College, Scranton, Pennsylvania, tape two modern mathematics lessons at St. John's the Evangelist Elementary School, Binghamton, May 1967.

EDUCATION

Vestal High School students are suspected of dumping this junk car on the front lawn of Union-Endicott High School, November 1967. The car was put there on the eve of the Vestal-U-E football game. The cheerleader is Leah Lotito, the U-E football queen.

COMMERCE

The Greater Binghamton region always thrived on commerce, and the 1940s, '50s and '60s were no exception. In many ways, those three decades were among the best times for the owners of small businesses.

The region was packed with family-owned grocery stores, shoe stores, jewelers and restaurants. Even then, business was constantly changing. The classic Red Robin Diner moved on down the road in 1958, picked up and trucked from its old Binghamton home to its new spot along Main Street in Johnson City.

Grand, old department stores celebrated anniversaries with parties for their employees, elegant hotels lined the city's bustling streets, and grocery stores staged price wars for the benefit of their milk customers. Businessmen tried anything, if they thought it might please the customer. One man tried his luck at becoming the only outdoor, year-round drive-in movie house in the region.

The photos in the Broome County Historical Society's archives show an economy that was booming along with the population. Mayors John Burns and Joseph Esworthy cut ribbons to celebrate grand openings. Politicians and developers posed with earth-moving equipment used to break ground for new shopping centers.

From the 21st century, it is easy to spot profound events that hardly drew any notice back then. In 1963, an up-and-coming company opened its 400th restaurant in Stow Flats, now the site of the Binghamton Plaza. Customers could drive up, get a meal and go about their business quickly at this new restaurant called McDonald's.

Walter Zagorsky appears ready to give Frank Kornprobst more than a trim as the two barbers ham it up to promote the 10th annual Broome County Barbers Association dinner-dance, April 1964 at the Sheraton Inn, Binghamton.

COMMERCE

Interior of Public Market, run by Endicott Johnson for the benefit of its employees, circa 1940.

Cora Glover and George Glezen inside Elmer Erickson's store, Upper Lisle, Triangle, circa 1940.

Chrysler/Plymouth showroom, Binghamton, 1941.

Employees from the 20 year club celebrate McLean's 60th anniversary, Binghamton, October 1941. Those known, front row: Ray Morris, Walter Dwight, Howard Parr, Mossman McLean, Charles Karns, William McLean, Jr., Ray Howe. Second row: Dick Blewer, Walter Roberts, Mrs. Walter Roberts, William McLean, Sr., Mable Barnes, John Burrell. Third row: Millis Vining, Dorothy Campbell, Myrtle Johnson, Hettie Kennedy and Floyd McLean.

SOUTHERN TIER MEMORIES: VOLUME II

Carlton Hotel on Chenango Street in Binghamton, June 1943.

Employees of the Wilson & Company meat market on Lewis Street, Binghamton, November 1947.

Del Rio Restaurant at 38 Hawley Street, Binghamton, circa 1944.

Interior of Planters Peanut store on Court Street, Binghamton, March 1944. Notice the unshelled peanuts strung to form canopy/wall covering.

COMMERCE

Businesses in the Goldsmith Block building on Court Street, Binghamton, December 1947.

Kresge store staff, October 15, 1945. Taken at the Bamboo Room of the Del Rio Restaurant. *Photo courtesy Mrs. Arlene Vosbury*

Interior of Conklin-Sullivan Seed Company on Washington Street, Binghamton, 1945.

Windsor Inn, Main Street in Windsor, June 1948.

Interior of the Windsor Inn on Main Street, June 1948.

Serafini Construction Company trucks, Binghamton, June 1948.

Wolfe's Garage and Studebaker Service, at 81 Washington Street, Binghamton, August 1948.

COMMERCE

Tickie's Restaurant at 1400 North Street, Endicott, June 1948.

Interior of the Red & White Grocery on Riverside Drive, Johnson City, August 1948.

Baby Bear Mart (South Side Grocery) at 49 South Washington Street, Binghamton, May 1948.

Mapes & Jacob moving company at the corner of State and Lewis Street, Binghamton, 1950.

Parlor City Shoe Company, Court Street, Binghamton, 1940s.

Exterior of the Red & White Grocery on Riverside Drive, Johnson City, August 1948.

George E. Treyz Trucking Company, Binghamton, March 1952.

COMMERCE

Display window at Sisson's department store, Court and State streets, Binghamton, September 1948.

Lunch counter at S.S. Kresge Company, 1950.

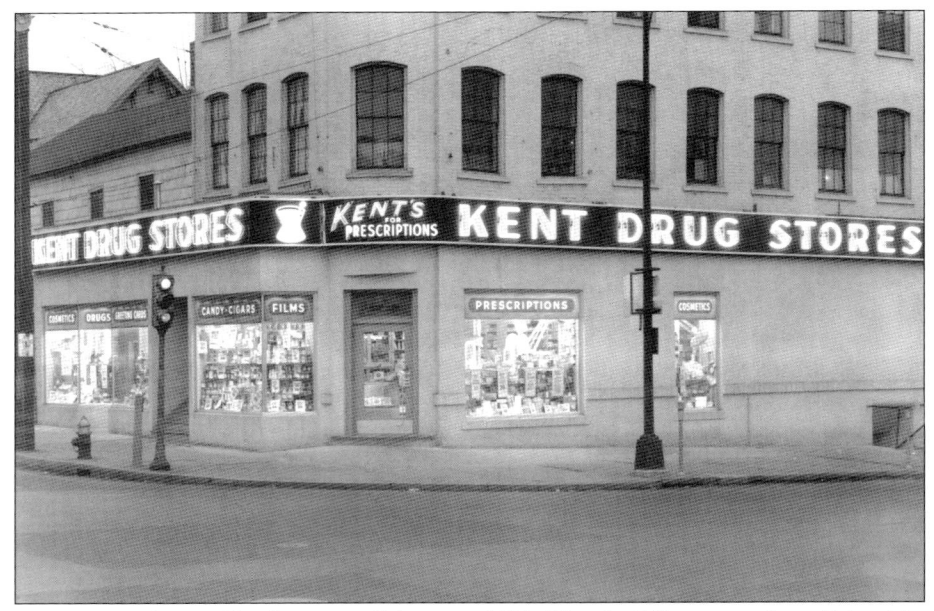

Kent Drug Store, Binghamton, February 1950. The building was demolished in 1997.

Interior of S.S. Kresge Company, 1950.

SOUTHERN TIER MEMORIES: VOLUME II

S.S. Kresge Company, Binghamton, 1950.

COMMERCE

Exterior of the Paint Bucket Store, Binghamton, June 1951.

Interior of the Paint Bucket Store, Binghamton, June 1951.

Joseph Brothers Furniture Store opened on South Washington Street, Binghamton, around June of 1950. The store was owned and operated by brothers George, William and Francis Joseph. *Courtesy Jennifer Ackerman*

Francis Joseph is sitting in his office at the Joseph Brothers Furniture store. *Courtesy Jennifer Ackerman*

The Hotel Arlington on Chenango Street, Binghamton, 1951. It was razed in 1968.

COMMERCE

Doug Johnson, head chef at the Johnson City Steak Shop, located at 66 North Broad Street, slices a ham, June 1961.

P & C market parking lot on Exchange and Prospect streets, Endicott, July 1961.

Olum's Clinton Street store proudly displays products of the 1900 Washer Company, 1948. The manufacturing company was founded in Binghamton, moved South and became the forerunner of the Whirlpool Corp.

SOUTHERN TIER MEMORIES: VOLUME II

Lobel's Store on Court Street, Binghamton, 1953.

Park Avenue Market at 105 Park Avenue, Binghamton, 1954.

McLean's Department Store, Perry Block, Binghamton, October 1957.

Canny's Trucking Company, Binghamton, April 1954.

COMMERCE

The Christmas display at the Fair Store featuring folks in a holiday setting. The displays were designed by James D. Morrison. *Courtesy Elizabeth B. Morrison*

The Christmas display at the Fair Store featuring folks in a kitchen setting. *Courtesy Elizabeth B. Morrison*

The Christmas display at the Fair Store featuring a large toy collection. *Courtesy Elizabeth B. Morrison*

The June display at the Fair Store featuring a bride and furnishings for her new home. *Courtesy Elizabeth B. Morrison*

Exterior of Callan-Major Jewelers on Chenango Street, Binghamton, 1954.

Deane Motor company, Plymouth and Chrysler dealers, Johnson City, 1959.

Interior of Callan-Major Jewelers, Binghamton, 1954.

First National Bank, Binghamton, 1950s.

COMMERCE

Exterior of the G & H Diner at Front and Franklin streets, Binghamton, 1959.

Cooks prepare a meal for a customer at the G & H Diner at Front and Franklin streets, Binghamton, 1959.

Red Robin Diner being moved from Binghamton to Johnson City in 1958. *Courtesy Mrs. Douglas Owen*

United Fund offices, Binghamton, April 1959. In the photo: Paul McFarland (in back office), left to right: Margaret A. Cook, Constance J. Cretser, Helen Kofira, Dorothy Burkholder, Ruth Hartley and Margaret Mitchell.

Sales girl shows off the merchandise to customers at Resnick's Women's Clothing store, Binghamton, 1960s.

The new "drive-in" hamburger restaurant known as McDonalds was nearing completion opposite the site of the new shopping center in Stow Flats, March 1963. In 1963, McDonald Corporation operated more than 400 hamburger stands in the United States.

COMMERCE

Binghamton Kosher Market at 84 Susquehanna Street, February 1962.

Sisson's department store at Court and State streets, Binghamton, 1962.

Roy M. Hanks, president of Georgia Hanks, in the new showroom at 235 Court Street, Binghamton, August 1966.

Mrs. Mary Welsh was among the first to use the services of Endicott National Bank's new "bankmobile," February 1963.

Thomas C. Butler, right, president of Grand Union Company and John M. O'Hara General Merchandise Manager getting ready to open up the new Grandway Store and Grand Union grocery store in the Binghamton Plaza, October 1963.

Richard Savage, assistant manager of the Court Street A & P store during price wars on milk (prices were down to 33 or 35 cents for half gallon), Binghamton, July 1963.

Mayor John J. Burns cuts the ribbon at the formal opening of the Public Service Garage addition at 297 Chenango Street, Binghamton, February 1963.

COMMERCE

Ground breaking for the shopping center at Five-Mile-Point which contained an A&P supermarket, branch office of First City National Bank and the Kirkwood Pharmacy. Pushing sheep's foot roller, left to right: Stewart D. Knowlton, one of the developers; George Koerber of Scranton, A&P vice-president; Stuart McCarty, a First-City vice-president; Malcolm Hunter, one of the developers; Glenn Willis, Kirkwood Assessor; in background, Robert E. Eggleston, Kirkwood Supervisor; George Hausmann, First-City public relations director; Chas. Jakatis and Michael Perhach, owners of the pharmacy; Stanley Turner, A&P assistant general division manager and the Reverend Robert H. Darling, Kirkwood Methodist minister.

Representatives of the Binghamton Plaza Merchant's Association look over the plans for the Plaza growth, 1964. Left to right: Randolph Parish, John O'Hara, Marian Boyd and Frederic Deyo.

George L. Thetga, left, owner of Kolb Electric at 8 Court Street, Binghamton, admires the plaque he is about to receive from Merton L. Beach, division manager of Onondaga Supply Company, Syracuse, distributor of Frigidaire appliances. The occasion was Frigidaire's 50th anniversary. Kolb Electric received an award for being the oldest Frigidaire dealer in the Triple Cities area.

Crowd hurries to get to "Dollar Days" at S.S. Kresge Company, August 1964.

Interior of Harry's Lunch restaurant. It moved from 144 State Street to 138 Washington Street in 1966.

COMMERCE

Winners of the "Shop Downtown Binghamton" contest prepare to board buses for their trip to Yankee Stadium, July 1964. Donald C. Oberhouser, assistant manager of the Binghamton Chamber of Commerce, fourth from right, checks winners on to the buses.

Felix M. Weisiger, Sr., vice-president of Endicott Johnson, checks over papers after signing the lease to open an Endicott Johnson shoe store in the new Endicott Plaza, August 1965. Those surrounding him are: Arthur W. Kennedy, Alfred Scafiero and standing, James W. Dowling.

Samuel C. Sunness, manager of the Airport Drive-in, ordered 600 car heaters in September 1961 so that his theater could become the only year-round outdoor movie house in the Triple Cities.

Binghamton Mayor Joseph W. Esworthy takes charge of the scissors during ribbon-cutting ceremonies for the opening of the new General Tire and Rubber Company service store at 383 State Street, October 1967. Left to right: Arthur Reilly, Girard E. Maloney and John J. Mullen.

Whitney Titus, left, and John A. Harris hang the new sign for the first doctor to practice in Colesville in over five years, July 1968.

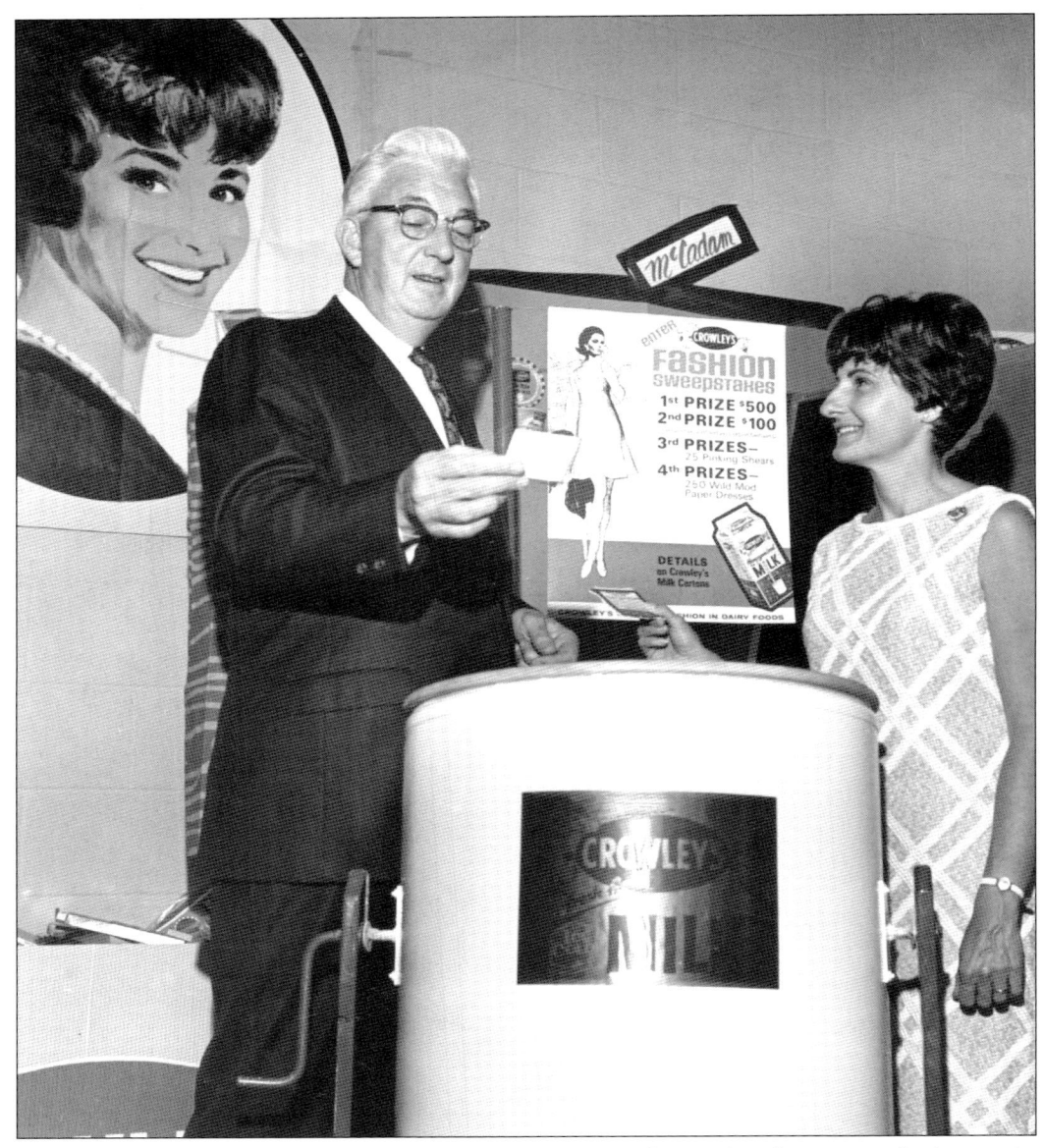

Mrs. Robert F. Boehm, food consultant for Crowley's Milk Co., hands names of winners in the Fashion Sweepstakes to company president Francis E. Crowley, June 1968. Donna Kerr of Montrose, Pa., won $500 worth of the latest fashions and Mrs. Wendell Greer of Owego won $100.

Misses Mary Watson, left, and Judith Baldwin help Dr. Charles N. Aswad, chairman of the Broome County Chamber of Commerce's Binghamton Council, explain what the chamber does in July 1966.

Andrew Lisi, 67, a bellhop at the Arlington Hotel for 27 years, assisted guests the weekend before the landmark hotel closed for good, June 1968.

Opening ceremonies for the Ethan Allen Carriage House, September 1969. Left to right: George J. Coury, Stanley Lush, Mrs. Coury, Roger Cooper, Reverend Paul W. Thompson, Joseph Monk, William Paynter and Mrs. Mary Calcagnini.

INDUSTRY

The backbone of the region's economy underwent seismic shifts as the population swelled, education improved and old ways gave way to new.

In 1951, Endicott Johnson Corp., ("EJ") perhaps the leading shoemaker in the world, employed 20,909 people. From this peak, the number of jobs steadily declined, bringing profound changes to the region. At one time, the company was a big draw for immigrants, acting as an engine to pump the Triple Cities full of people willing to work hard, even if they had scant education.

As EJ entered its twilight years, other corporations were growing rapidly. IBM, already a behemoth, would get bigger. Universal Instruments and Link Technologies would grow under the leadership of such men as J. Donald Ahearn and Edwin A. Link. These companies, as they adapted to new technologies, needed better-educated employees.

During these years, many jobs were tied to the defense industry. World War II, the long struggle with Communism, the Korean War, and the first shots of the Vietnam War created thousands of jobs in the factories and laboratories of the region. IBM built a huge defense plant in Owego, EJ made shoes for the troops, and other factories hummed with the war effort.

Employees of the Beemer Products Corp., March 1952.

INDUSTRY

Employees of Remington Rand leave the Westover plant, circa 1940. The plant is now part of the BAE Aerospace operation.

Endicott Johnson food personnel gather, circa 1940.

Endicott Johnson President Charles F. Johnson Jr. poses with a party group, circa 1940.

Office workers at IBM Endicott, circa 1940.

INDUSTRY

A drill press operator works at Universal Instruments, October 1947.

Employees of Universal Instruments, 1943. Company president J. Donald Ahearn is third from right in the front row.

The Villecco Cheese Factory, circa 1945. Left to right: Billy Villecco, unidentified man, Joe Villecco, Dominick Villecco and Louis Villecco, Sr.
Photo courtesy Tony Villecco

An employee of Crowley Milk monitors equipment, circa 1950.

Employees of Endicott Johnson meet with president Charles F. Johnson, Jr., 1952.

Mills A. MacQueen, president of Drybak Corp., presents 25-year-service awards to employees, December 1952. From left: Eva Weber, Bertha Witteburt, Mary Marano, Mary Santoni, and Mildred MacCrabie.

Workers at McIntosh Engineering Laboratories, March 1952.

INDUSTRY

The office women of the McKay operation of Endicott Johnson gathered for a Christmas celebration, 1952. Pictured are Viva Felton, Sally Roberts, Bess Turk, Mary Barcay, Pat O'Connell, Pat Burdick, Elsie Ticknor, Marion Arnold, Evelyn Brutevan, Lorretta Savage and Jean Herzog.

In May 1953, an airborne photographer captured the Endicott Johnson Shoe Co. factories, the CFJ Park with its huge swimming pool, the Public Market and surrounding homes of EJ workers.

Civil Defense officials present an award to Felters Corp., Johnson City, July 1953. From left: State CD director Lt. General, Clarence R. Huebner, county CD executive director, Robert R. Douglass, Felters plant manager, Paul E. Waltz, and plant safety director, Fred W. Cooke.

Ansco employees Fritz Majercik, Wes Gerdus, Harold Harsh, Elton Beavan, Rudi Majercik and George Mertaugh, 1954.

The interior of Link Aviation.

INDUSTRY

Inside the Platt and Wren Optical Co., 163 Washington Street, Binghamton, circa 1958.

Joseph H. Murphy, director of the New York Tax Commission, demonstrates the new IBM "brain," January 1959. The machine uses punch cards to check returns for cheating and honest mistakes.

Construction is underway on IBM's mammoth new defense plant in Owego, August 1956.

IBM-Endicott employees flood the streets outside a plant, circa 1960.

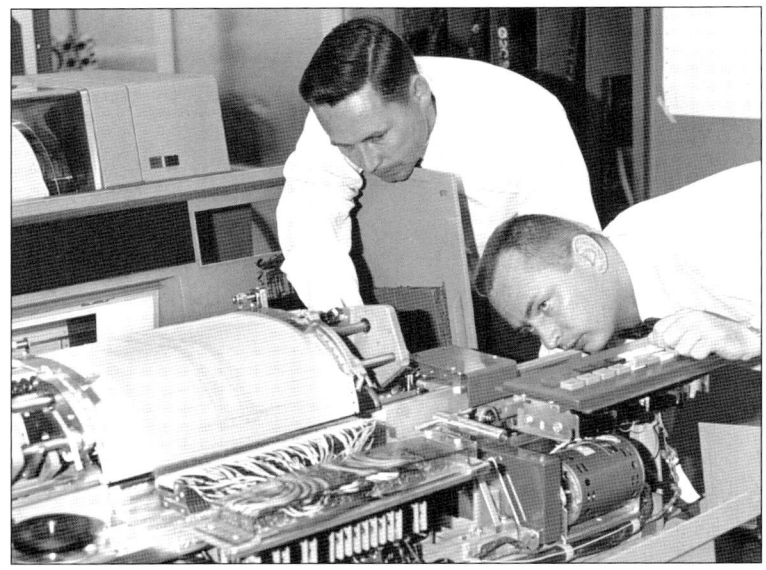

INDUSTRY

Charles Woodruff and F.W. Martin, IBM engineers, check the workings of the new bar printer, October 1962. The pair helped develop the printer.

The Clark-Cleveland Co. of Binghamton made a variety of powdered products. They made a paste to fasten false teeth and a poison that killed lice. The Army liked the lice product so much that the government gave the company priority on obtaining packaging materials, which it could also use for its other products. Pictured here is chemist Donald Germann.

P.J. Casella, center, president and chief executive officer of E.J. Corp., points out the locations of old shoe factories in the Triple Cities before a meeting at which business leaders and an economist discussed Broome's economic future. At the January 1963 meeting were: seated: Philip Hammer of Hammer Associates, Casella, and Wayne W. Cawley, president of Cadre Industries Corp. Standing are Frank G. Paul, general manager of IBM-Endicott; William W. Wood Jr., president of Simulation and Control Group of General Precision; W. Wallace McDowell, resident vice president of IBM-Endicott; Robert M. Verburg, general manager Ansco-Ozalid; and William J. Kuehl, general manager of General Electric, Westover.

Ralph Fedder, (center left), manager of the Fine Welt Plant is congratulated for his plant's quality, 1963. Endicott Johnson Corp. offered a contest to improve quality. He is being congratulated by Edward Shultz, Men's Dress Shoe Assembly Division manager. Holding the banner are Quality Control Director, Ted Lemoncelli and campaign director, Charles H. Bauer.

Miss Annalee Robbins works at the new IBM 1240 computer system that was installed at the Endicott National Bank, 1964. Left to right: H. Kenneth McQueen, bank president; Arthur J. Capp, manager Endicott IBM sales office; and Ernie A. Hoff, bank auditor.

INDUSTRY

These eight IBM employees are among dozens who obtained master's degrees at the Endicott-Owego Center of Syracuse University, June 1964. Pictured in front are: Clement K. Margolf, James J. Rooney, Edward T. Lynch, and Gerald N. West. In rear are: Robert M. Decker, William B. Firstenberg, Paul E. Johnson and Donald L. Sheppard.

A workman puts final touches on a sign at Five-Mile Point as J. Karl Meyer, right, and Robert Rice look on, November 1964.

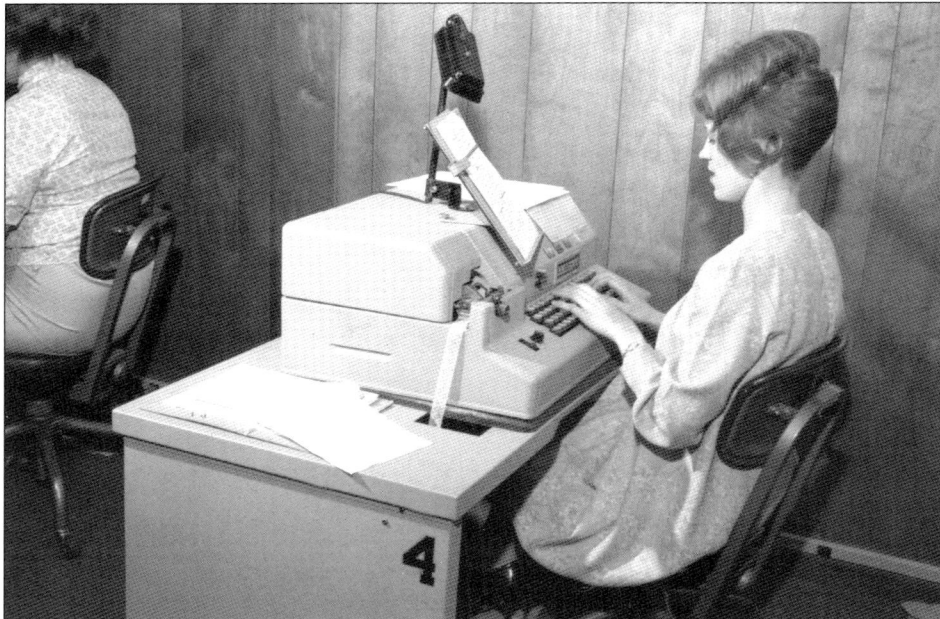

A typist prepares a paper tape for typesetting at Vail Ballou, 1968.

Link Athletic Club members are surrounded by gifts they are stacking up for the annual Christmas Party, November 1967. The party was for children of the employees of the Link Group of General Precision and held at the West End Armory. Foreground Club President Carl A. Paccio. Left to right in center of picture: Vice President, Leo Bucci, Vice President, Michael Straka, Thomas Wilber and Emagene Kennan. Top: Frank Lance and Betty Rogers.

MILITARY

If you study the photos in the archives of the Broome County Historical Society, you will see that Greater Binghamton contributed mightily to the nation's war and defense efforts. This was not a one-way street: Money flowed from the Pentagon into the region's factories, employing thousands of people.

Endicott Johnson factories made more than 1 million pairs of boots for troops in Vietnam. Ed Link's factories built airplane simulators that saved many pilots' lives by preventing training accidents.

Broome residents, like all Americans, eagerly signed up to serve in World War II, when the nation fought a protracted, two-ocean war for survival. More than 20,000 Broome men and women entered the service. An estimated 625 of them were killed or left missing in action.

This was total war. Even in Broome, residents scanned the skies for enemy planes, and gathered scrap and other material for the defense effort. When Japan surrendered, the good news propelled many into the streets for extended celebrations.

Still, the nation's struggles could bring unbearable sadness home. In 1966, a World War I veteran died after composing a memorial to his son, killed in Vietnam. Loved ones had to endure two simultaneous funerals.

Winds of protest began to stir in the last part of the 1960s, as some residents, especially those at the State University of New York at Binghamton, became disillusioned with the Vietnam War.

Louis Lowenstein and Louis Hartman built casings for the Tiny Tim Rocket, demonstrated by the Defense Department, December 1946. The demonstration was part of the unveiling of a proving ground in California. Pictures of the rocket being launched from a railroad type track are featured in an article carried by the Binghamton Press.

MILITARY

Civilians helped watch the skies for enemy planes during the early days of World War II. Standing at their rooftop observation post on Oakdale Road are Laurella Barnum (Christensen) and Marjory Barnum (Hinman). The 4H girls watched and reported on Saturdays after a training period.

Johnson City World War II scrap drive, 1940s.

Crowds mill around Court and Chenango streets after news of Japan's surrender, August 1945. In all of World War II, an estimated 620 Broome County residents were killed or declared missing in action. More than 20,000 men and women were in uniform during the war.

SOUTHERN TIER MEMORIES: VOLUME II

Couples dance in the street after news of Japan's surrender reaches Binghamton, August 1945.

MILITARY

Three World War II heroes, circa 1945. Left to right: Thomas Watson, who served in the US Army for 20 years, was a POW of the Japanese and survived the Bataan Death March. Thomas Maher was a US Navy radioman on the USS Essex. William Maher, who served in the US Army Air Corps, was shot down over France and was a POW of the Germans. *Courtesy James Foley*

Two Marines and a Coast Guardsman stage a mock battle on the vessel which took them to Iwo Jima, one of the bloodiest battles of World War II, 1945. The referee is Coast Guardsman Philip Vanderbeck, who was a Binghamton patrolman before entering the service. Vanderbeck later became a legendary chief of Binghamton detectives. Vanderbeck was a two-time winner of the Binghamton Press' Golden Gloves contests as a welterweight. With gloves are William Minoia of Binghamton and George M. Merrill of Johnson City. At Iwo Jima, Merrill was wounded in the left arm and leg. Minoia was killed February 19, 1945.

Bernie Massar home from the service in the late 1940s with his best friend, "Ace." *Courtesy Donna M. Massar*

Electrician Mate First Class Kenneth Lason, right, receives his quarterly check at the first pay call of Binghamton Division 3-47, Naval Reserve, January 1947. Pay officers are Ensign James R. Buckle, left and Andrew Rosics, storekeeper disbursing mate, first class.

Members of the 48th Special Infantry Company, Binghamton-based Marine reserve unit, July 1954. Left to right: Cpl. John S. Hill, Owego; Pfc. James S. Philpott, Jr., Oxford; Pfc, Howard E. Riner, Binghamton; Pfc. James C. Kaelin; Pfc, Guy S. Lougheed, Oxford; and Pfc. Francis J. Kane, Binghamton.

Mayor Walker B. Lounsberry signs a proclamation to make Navy Day official in Binghamton, October 1948. Standing are: Chief Petty Officer Harold H. Moore, left, of the Binghamton Navy Recruiting Station and Lieutenant Commander M.L. Skelton, officer in charge of the Binghamton Naval Reserve Training Center.

MILITARY

Marines from the Binghamton-based 48th Rifle Company of the Marine Corps Reserves load "Project Christmas Star" packages bound for servicemen in Viet Nam. Left to right: Lance Corporal Thomas Harder, PFC Salvatore Talamo and Gy. Sgt. Robert A. Hiles.

Colonel Leon G. Payes, commanding officer of 73rd Field Hospital at Army Reserve Center in Hillcrest, receives a piece of cake from Captain Janet L. Parson, chief nurse at the hospital, January 1964. The event marked the 62nd birthday of the Nurse Corps. Behind Colonel Payes is Lieutenant Colonel Robert Orcutt.

A sad double military funeral was held for two members of Binghamton's Johnson family, March 1966. Hospital Corpsman Lawrence Everett Johnson, 26, was killed by a bullet in Vietnam. Seamen Randall Wike and Robert Molessa guard his casket. In the background is the casket of the soldier's father, Everett Johnson, 67, a World War I veteran who died after composing the memorial for his son's funeral.

MILITARY

General W. M. Mantz honors Guy Zonio, a veteran Endicott Johnson employee, for the company's production of the 1,000,000 boots for use by troops in Vietnam, February 1969. The general, commander of the Defense Personnel Support Center in Philadelphia, accepted the boots at a ceremony at the Boys and Youth Plant in Johnson City.

Members of the third Battalion 392nd Regiment of the U.S. Army Reserves cram duffle bags for the annual two-week training stint at Fort Dix, New Jersey, July 1965. At left is Sergeant George W. Tompkins, and SFC John A. Jones, both of Binghamton.

Student Timothy Smith leads other students in song before the start of an anti-Vietnam Teach-in held in the lobby of the administration building at the State University in Binghamton, February 1968. *Courtesy Press and Sun Bulletin Archives*

PUBLIC SERVICE

Many Broome residents were devoted public servants, who helped protect the health and safety of thousands of their neighbors.

Polio was a scourge not wiped out until the 1960s, when the Salk and Sabin vaccines defeated the terrible disease. As late as 1964, polio struck Broome residents, and doctors and public health nurses worked hard to eradicate the killer.

Men entered police departments and began long careers protecting the public. The Society's photos captured two men who would become chiefs many years later: George Korutz in Johnson City, the father of the current chief, Stephen Korutz, and John Sejan, Jr. in Binghamton.

The 1960s were the height of the Cold War, and Civil Defense was a pressing concern. Police offered training sessions with gas masks. Senior authorities drew up plans to estimate how far radiation would spread if a nuclear bomb struck.

Those concerned with the well-being of the community had to cope with the demands of a rising population. Vestal installed new drinking-water wells. The federal government built a big new post office in Binghamton. Every agency had to buy new equipment.

Some things never change. Adults love playing Santa Claus to children. And business and government leaders will meet to discuss lowering the cost of local government.

Fire Bureau Lieutenant Robert J. Maloney briefs three fire inspectors at the start of the annual inspection of Binghamton homes for fire hazards, 1956. Left to right: Fireman John N. Conomikes, Lieutenant Maloney and firemen William F. Thomas and Michael Rusin, Jr.

Central fire station, Carroll Street, Binghamton, 1948.

The Broome County Board of Supervisors and local businessmen met to discuss the structure and costs of local government, March 1949. Seated are supervisors Edwin M. Jones, Port Dickinson; Chairman F. Clyde Eggleston, Barker; Samuel H. Pearis and Earl J. Daniels. Standing are: Claude M. Sherman, J. Donald Ahearn, George E. Knowlton, Kenneth I. VanCott and supervior Earl S. Lindsey.

Vestal's councilman, William W. Castle, center, goes over the agenda of the organization meeting with Justice of the Peace Leland Morton, left, and Town Clerk Lester O. Kretschmar, January 1951.

Unidentified firemen hold a new-type nozzle which sprayed water over a vast area to douse fires, October 1951.

PUBLIC SERVICE

Johnson City Police Chief, Floyd L. Allen, center, help Patrolman Anthony Kovac, left, Johnson City Police Association president, and Sergeant Harry Pettit check final arrangements for the village's annual Police Ball at East Branch EJAA Recreation Center, November 1953.

Vote counting for Outstanding Citizen of Port Dickinson, Hillcrest, November 1954. Seated, left, William G. Hill, General Chairman.

Chenango Bridge men teamed up to give a fresh coat of paint and trim to the community's Civic Center building, 1953. More than 20 volunteers climbed up ladders loaned by community residents.

84

John Linehan of Johnson City, receives congratulations from officials as he and 51 other members of Johnson City's auxiliary police unit receive Civil Defense Accreditation in ceremonies at the Chester J. Jaskiewicz American Legion Clubhouse on Prospect Street, 1952. Left to right: Johnson City Mayor, Donald E. Stocum; Police Chief, Floyd L. Allen; Mr. Linehan, and Police Lieutenant, Alfred Lamphere, deputy director.

Mrs. Helen R. Moriarity, a service assistant for the New York Telephone Company is teaching Binghamton police how to operate their new switchboard, April 1953. Watching the operation are Lieutenant John V. Gillen, left, and Patrolman John F. Cooney.

PUBLIC SERVICE

Endicott Patrolman Ernest Pittarelli stands guard in Main Street to give a schoolboy safe passage across the Loder Avenue intersection, May 1954.

Captain Michael F. O'Neil, left and Lieutenant Julius Buchinsky use a ballistic comparison microscope in the Binghamton Police Bureau's crime laboratory, April 1954.

County Board of Supervisors, Binghamton, 1955. Front row: Thomas J. Conlon, Samuel J. Cucci, Clarence Walter, Edward J. Moran, Henry Baldwin, Miss Marie J. Pangburn, Account Clerk; Mrs. Iris Gaige, Secretary to County Attorney; Robert M. Ford, Chairman; Mrs. Margaret Wallace, Assistant to Deputy Clerk; Miss Ruth E. Spencer, Deputy Clerk; Howard Davis, Clerk. Board of Supervisors: John E. Ash, G. Earle Personius, George J. Macko, H. Chester Larrabee. Second Row: Howard M. Smith, Justin C. Flannigan, Assistant County Attorney; Carl R. Bird, Charles A. Root, E.M. Jones, William D. Bennett, Walter F. Ayres, Joseph M. Daugherty, Harry D. Prew, Leland L. Jones, Earl S. Lindsey, Erford G. Barrows, Harold B. Christian, Lynn T. West, Claude A. Wheeler, W.H. Johnson, Jr., Lewis M. Evans, Walter S. Randall.

PUBLIC SERVICE

Johnson City Patrolmen George Korutz, left, and John Zenzel look over loot taken from the Frank A. Johnson Post 758, American Legion clubhouse by two 14-year-old boys, 1955. The two youths were hurt when a blank .30 caliber shell, one of approximately 150 taken from the clubhouse, exploded as they detonated it with a rock.

Willard H. Lamphere, right, Broome County chief deputy director of civil defense, presents certificates to three graduates of the State Rescue Training School, Binghamton, 1955. Left to right: Harold F. Griffin and Walter M. Pilotti, firemen, both of Binghamton Fire Bureau and Earl G. Snyder, assistant deputy director of rescue for county civil defense.

Edwin Lyon, left and Richard Keane prepare Christmas cards and other mail for sorting into the proper pigeonholes, Binghamton, December 1954.

Binghamton Fire Bureau's new addition, May 1957. Left to right, foreground: Fire Chief Frank J. Buckman, Mayor Donald W. Kramer and Fire Training Instructor John A. Sedor. Firemen in rear are: Walter Pilotti, Thomas Burns, Harvey Chaffee and Lieutenant Robert Cohn.

Aerial view of the Broome County Courthouse, Binghamton, circa 1956.

An artesian well pumps more than 1,000 gallons of pure water per minute as Town of Vestal officials gather around to check its speed, May 1958. Left to right: Bernard Pierson, councilman; Leland Morton, Town of Vestal Justice of Peace; Harley Murphy, water superintendent, and Schuyler Stewart, representative of Stewart Brothers, Inc. water supply contractors.

PUBLIC SERVICE

Police and newsmen met at the Paramount Diner, March 1959, Binghamton to discuss crime, fires and accidents. Left to right, seated: Donald H. Rodman, Port Dickinson police and fire chief, and Floyd Avis, Broome County sheriff's deputy. Standing: Binghamton Assistant Police Chief, Joseph W. Sullivan; Endicott Police Sergeant, Joseph Carosella; *Binghamton Press* managing editor and panel moderator, Erwin C. Cronk; Press Photographer and police-press relations chairman for Region 2, National Press Photographers Association, Paul K. Konecny; and , WNBF-TV cameraman and chapter president, Tony Baxewanis.

Patrolman Peter J. Slack, Johnson City meter maintenance man, tries out the new meter truckster purchased by the village, May 1962.

Repair and maintenance of Endicott's 860 meters in 1962 was a full-time job for Patrolman Lawrence Nabinger.

PUBLIC SERVICE

Bottom row, left to right: Binghamton Police Chief Joseph W. Sullivan, Mayor John J. Burns, Lieutenant Jerome W. McCarthy and Detective Paul DiNardo stand in front of City Hall with four members of the Police Bureau who received promotions, July 1964. In uniforms, left to right: Lieutenant Edmund T. Covaleski, Captain John J. Blaha, Captain Richard A. Bernard and Detective John Sejan, Jr.

Binghamton Patrolman John Sejan Jr., tries out one of the new fleet of ten cars purchased for the police bureau, March 1960.

Johnson City Traffic Officer Alfred Lamphere inspects the new 1963 Dodge station wagon-ambulance delivered to the village.

Broome County declared war on driver apathy, June 1963. First Assistant District Attorney Herbert A. Kline speaks about the dangers of driver apathy to magistrates and police in the grand jury room of the courthouse at the opening of an emergency traffic safety campaign. Seated in the front row are LeLand E. Morton, deputy state motor vehicle commissioner; Delbert Pembridge, Endicott police chief; and Sgt. Russell Evans, sheriff's department.

Christmas rush at the Endicott Post Office, 1964.

Binghamton's meter maids donned new seersucker summer uniforms, June 1964. Pictured are Nicki Keane, Betty Broking and Rita Shiptenko. A fourth employee, Jean Tacey is not pictured.

PUBLIC SERVICE

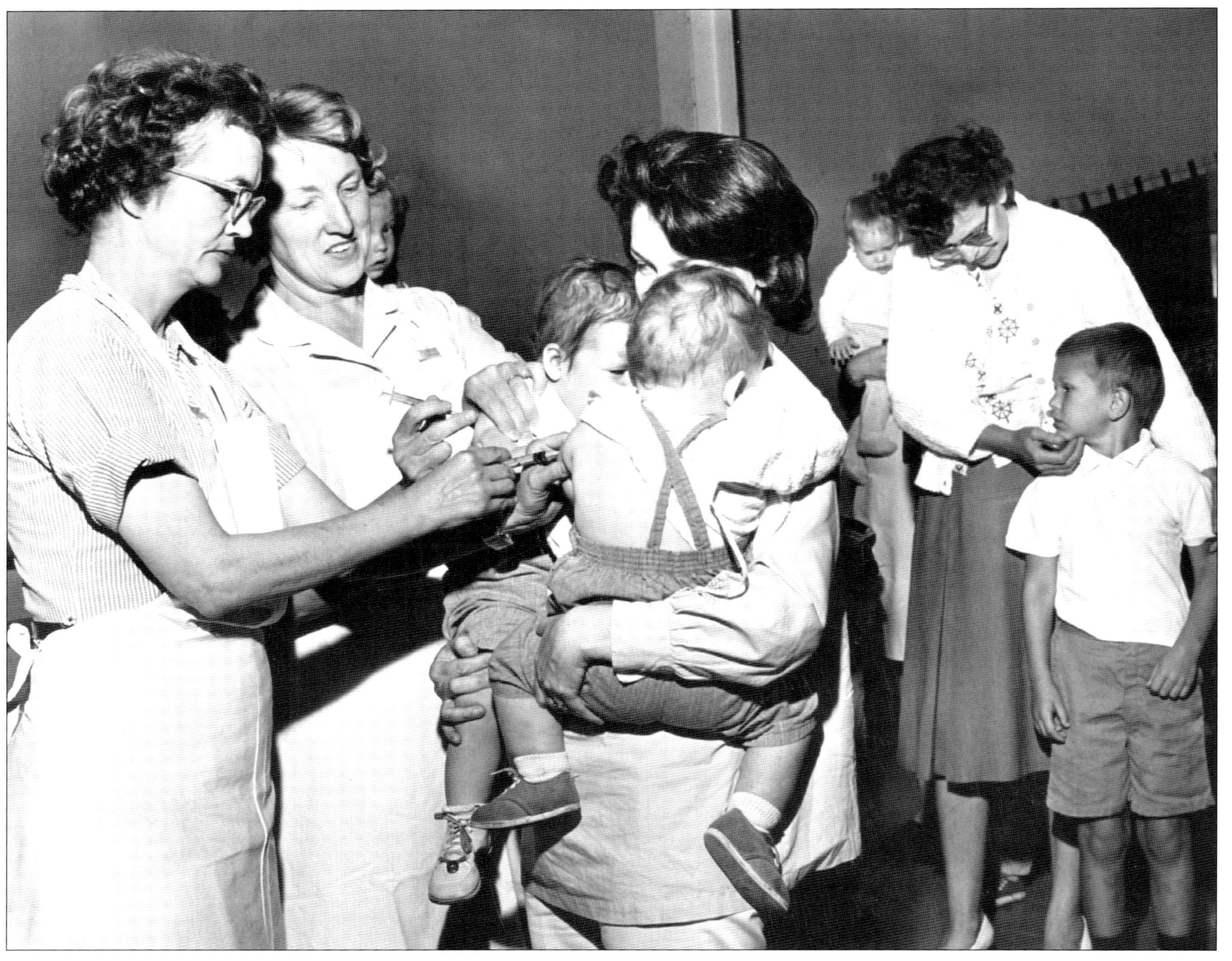

The first suspected case of polio in two years prompted a run on Salk vaccinations, August 1964. Public health nurses Rita McKeon and Madelon Alger give shots to twins Kim and Todd Thorpe of Endicott. Holding the 16-month-olds is their mother, Mrs. Karl Thorpe.

The Sabin oral polio vaccine eventually replaced the Salk vaccine, given by injection, and communities began receiving shipments of the new treatment. This shipment arrived at Binghamton General Hospital and was checked by Dr. Jason K. Moyer, Mrs. Nearle H. Cobb and Dr. John F. Spring, September 1964.

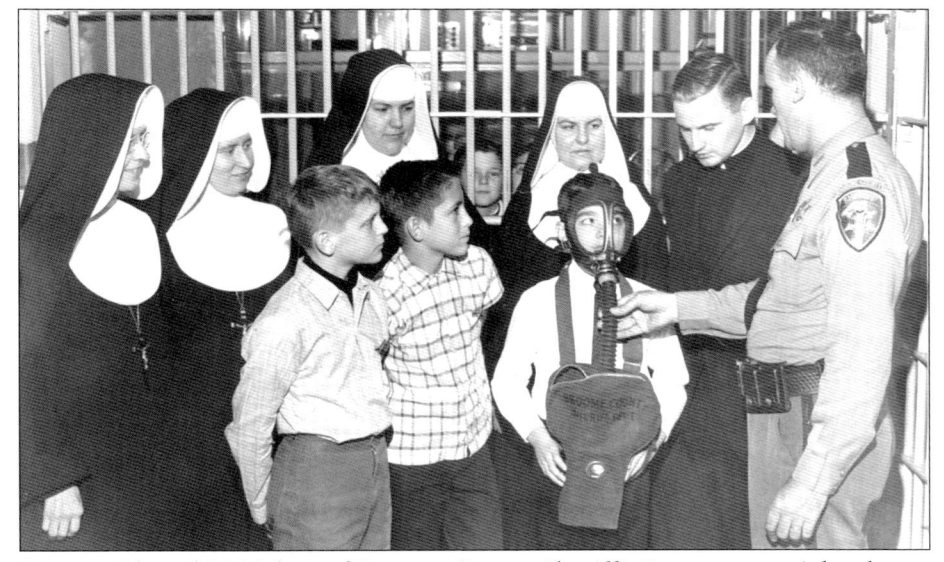

Deputy Edward M. Molnar of Broome County Sheriff's Department, right, shows three junior deputies from St. Ann's School a gas mask during a visit of the school's patrol boys and girls to the county office, November 1965. Left to right, first row: Michael Pochily, Daniel Harendza, Joseph Gaube, and Deputy Molnar. Second row: Sister Mary David, Sister Mary Hope, Sister Mary Patricia and Sister Mary Julie, all sisters of SS Cyril and Methodius and Reverend Alfred J. Bebel.

Dante A. Tomassi, Binghamton's first dog warden and a new panel truck in front of City Hall, May 1967.

PUBLIC SERVICE

Mailing cards from Glen Aubrey Post Office to Maryland in commemoration of the Pony Express, August, 1966.

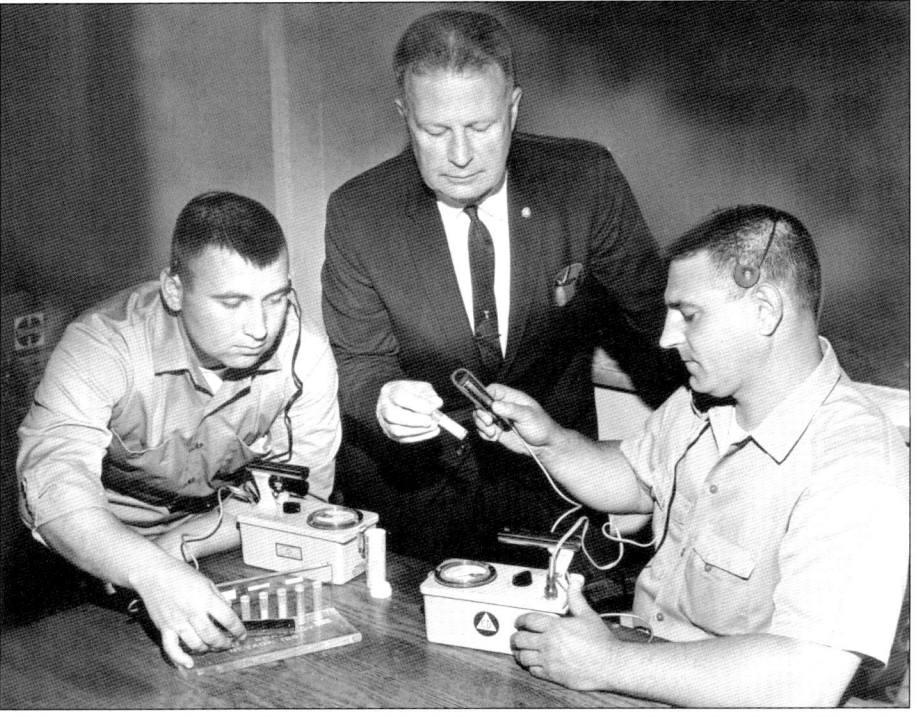

William Macan, left, and Raymond Redolphy, members of the Endicott Fire Department completed a 20-hour course in the study of radiological emergency operations taught by Enoch O. Glesne, center, of the Cornell University Extension Civil Defense Program, May 1966.

Mr. and Mrs. B. Browe Stone inside the Corbettsville Post Office, October 1965.

Binghamton Post Office on Henry Street under construction, July 1967.

Members of the Special Weapons Defense Service of the Broome County Civil Defense Organization discuss new methods for predicting the intensity of radioactive fallout in case a nuclear bomb would fall in New York. Pictured are: Corporal Timothy H. Murphy, a field representative of the state civil defense commission; E. Stanley Moser, chief of the plotting section of the Broome organization; Carl E. Johnson, an assistant to Moser; and Dr. Frank J. Kasuba, director of the service.

Broome County Sheriff enforcement vehicle, Binghamton, circa 1967.

PUBLIC SERVICE

During a talk on fire safety at MacArthur Elementary School, Inspector Howard F. Orcutt imparts a few words of caution to Karen Kozlowski and Martha Moore, Binghamton 1968.

Two-year-old Jimmy Nash rides in the Binghamton firemen's picket line in front of his father, Fireman D.J. Nash, November 1968.

Emile Clavey, left, chairman of the Main Board of Fire Commissioners, hands Fire Chief Leonard Bullock the keys to the new pumper in December 1968.

Ralph D. Philpott, contractor on the Post Office building at Bible School Park, hands over the key to the new building to Martin H. Crippen, postmaster, November 1968. Looking on is Reverend M.C. Patterson, President of School. The school had its own mailing address and post office for many years.

William E.D. Barlow who succeeded Lester O. Kretschmar as Vestal's town clerk, talks to Mrs. Ralph G. Ormiston, who replaced Mrs. Kretschmar as deputy town clerk, March 1968. The Kretschmars retired after many years of service.

PUBLIC SERVICE

Vestal Supervisor John W. Hudanich hands over the keys to a newly-delivered tanker truck to Fire Chief Fred W. Singer at the Fire Company 1 station on North Main Street. Looking on are assistant chiefs William Decker, left and Roy Stehm.

Broome County Sheriff John Perhach watches while Amy Carey, 6, sits on Santa's lap at the Wyoming Conference Home, December 1969. Handing out presents in the background are deputies Joseph DeRosa, John Gavula, and John Goodrich. Santa is played by Harry Bloomer of Johnson City.

PUBLIC SERVICE

Vestal's top fire officials with specially equipped emergency squad truck, December 1969. Left to right: Chief William F. Oliver, assistant chief William E. Decker, Roy Stehm and Fred Singer.

TRANSPORTATION

Life speeded up for residents of Greater Binghamton as the region discarded old ways of transportation in favor of the quicker airplanes and more convenient automobiles.

The Penn-Can Highway, now known as Interstate 81, opened in 1961, allowing motorists to jump on the new national highway system. Airplanes became bigger, safer, faster, and the traditional passenger railroads faded into nostalgia.

In 1955, crowds packed the Lackawanna station in Binghamton, waiting to board the luxury train Phoebe Snow. By 1966, that era had ended. In between, the Broome County Airport, on a hilltop in the Town of Maine, roared to life.

At the start of the period, it was rare for a family to own a car. By the end of the 1960s, almost every family had one, if not two, cars. This shift had profound effects on the traditional city as people started moving to the suburbs.

The rise of the individual auto made it difficult for private commuter bus lines to hang on, and soon Broome County, already in the airport business, was taking over the intra-county bus lines.

The shift began a new tradition: local leaders started meeting to improve traffic flow along the Vestal Parkway, a quest that may never end.

Opening of the Penn-Can Highway, August 1961.

TRANSPORTATION

People and Blue Motor Coach Line buses line Henry Street, Binghamton.

Turntable, a mighty merry-go-round for giant engines, at the Delaware and Hudson yards in Binghamton, 1946.

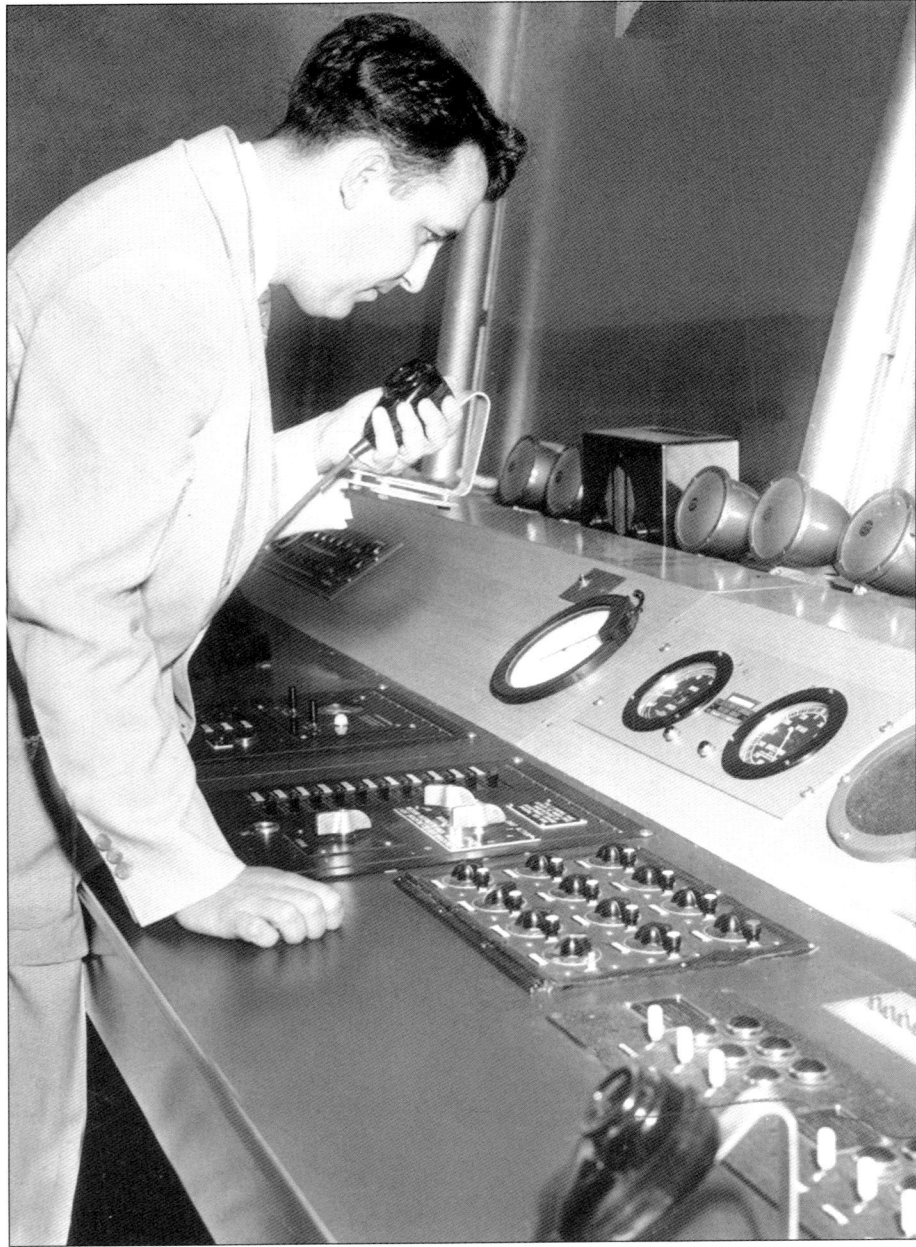

Louis F. Leon, chief airways operation specialist at the Broome County Airport, gives wind speed and direction by radio to a plane requesting information, August 1951.

TRANSPORTATION

Triple Cities Traction Corporation bus drivers agreement signed by Albert Schreiber, TCTC vice-president and Leonard S. Miller, business agent for the union, Binghamton, 1950s.

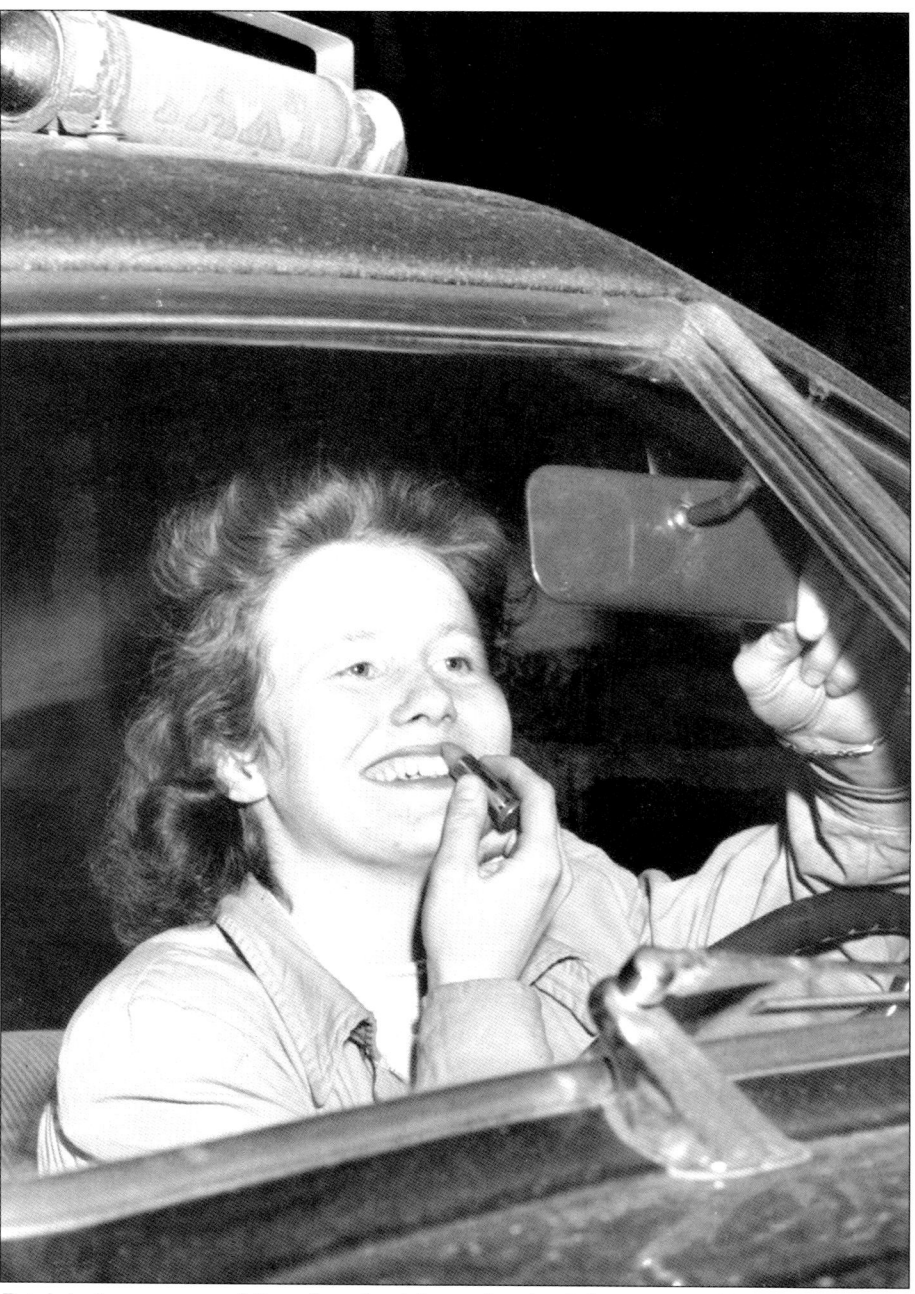

Patricia Lyons, one of four female drivers for the Johnson City Taxi Co., primps before going out for a fare, January 1949.

Howard W. Ostrom, Johnson City resident, was promoted by Mohawk Airlines in 1953, while he was recovering in Arnot Ogden Memorial Hospital from an auto accident. Pictured upon his arrival are, from left: First Officer, Ray Hitt; Mohawk Airlines chief pilot, Captain Ralph Bower; Mr. and Mrs. Ostrom and George L. Bright.

TRANSPORTATION

Six new cabs were delivered to the Binghamton Taxicab Company at a cost of $18,000 in 1959. Harry A. Miller, Jr., (foreground) is the only one identified.

Broome County Airport, August 1959.

Crowd waits for a ride on the streamliner Phoebe Snow luxury train in Binghamton, circa 1955.

Binghamton mail is ready for transfer at the Lackawanna railroad station, 1960.

TRANSPORTATION

Paul Jones, Endicott, an agent for the Erie-Lackawanna railroad, November 1966.

One last train ride from Binghamton to Albany on December 5, 1963 was enjoyed by, left to right: Mrs. John O'Brien, Mrs. James Shea and Mrs. John Conrad.

Western Broome County officials and businessmen gather at the ribbon that was to be cut to mark the opening of the Thomas J. Watson Sr., Bridge. Among those pictured are: Herbert R. Levine, Mayor E. Raymond Lee, Arthur K. Watson and Edwin L. Crawford.

SOUTHERN TIER MEMORIES: VOLUME II

Not even flooding on Henry Street could stop the Short Line bus from going through Binghamton, July 1964.

TRANSPORTATION

Pheobe Snow, the last Erie-Lackawana passenger train to depart from Binghamton, leaves the station, November 1966.

SOUTHERN TIER MEMORIES: VOLUME II

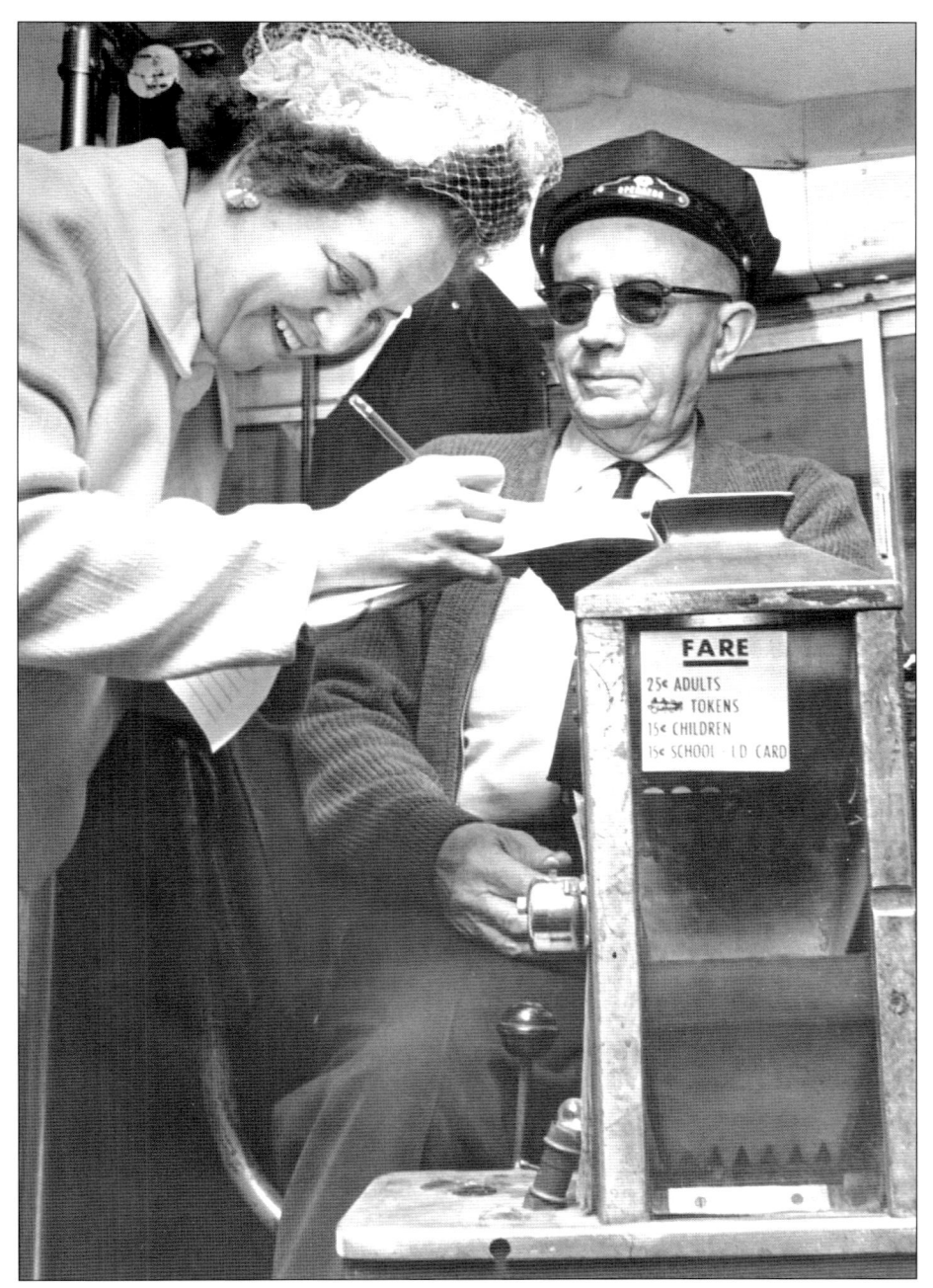

Lois Richards signs a petition urging Broome County to take over the Triple Cities Traction Corporation as Roland H. Welliner, driver, looks on, April 1968.

Edwin L. Crawford, chairman of supervisors, Broome County bus system, is coached by driver Ralph Osborne, June 1968.

TRANSPORTATION

Gerald W. Winston shows off an executive plane, the type his new company planned to produce, at the Broome County Airport, July 1967.

Committee of Vestal residents and businessmen that organized at the Skylark Diner to fight certain proposed state changes in the Vestal Parkway East traffic flow and parking pattern, April 1967. Left to right: Joel A. Scelsi, Patsy Scarano, William B. Mullen, James H. Westfall, Jr., Orval L. Stevens, Warren F. Schroeder and John Vokulich.

Inauguration of Broome County bus service to Windsor. Left to right: Robert Schrader, County Executive Edwin L. Crawford and Windsor Mayor Charles Rock, September 1969.

Engine No. 759 during the Centennial of the High Iron Company in 1969.

SOCIETY

While change buffeted many areas of life, traditional religions remained the focus for many in Broome County. The buildings we worshipped in changed dramatically as the population grew, but the spiritual beliefs were steadfast.

New churches opened at a rapid clip. Almost every denomination needed a new building or improvements to their old building. Impressive new churches on Clinton Street and elsewhere opened.

Religious schools were built. Probably the most dramatic example was the new $1.5 million Catholic Central High School in Binghamton on the grounds of the old St. Mary's Home. In 1976, the school combined with Endicott's Seton High.

The generation that won World War II was a generation of joiners. They swelled the ranks of the American Legion, service clubs and political organizations.

One of the subtexts in this period was how women identified themselves. Almost all the married women used their husband's names when speaking with photographers.

Graduation group at the Israel Synagogue, Binghamton, May 1964.

Vestal Center Baptist Church Bible School in 1947. *Photo courtesy Darcie Hotaling Gottschall*

Lewis Lyons, standing, chants over the wine at Children's Seder, the annual rehearsal for Passover at Temple Israel, Binghamton, April 1948. Leon Segal, principal of the United Hebrew Schools, is at right.

High Street Methodist Church, Binghamton, March, 1948.

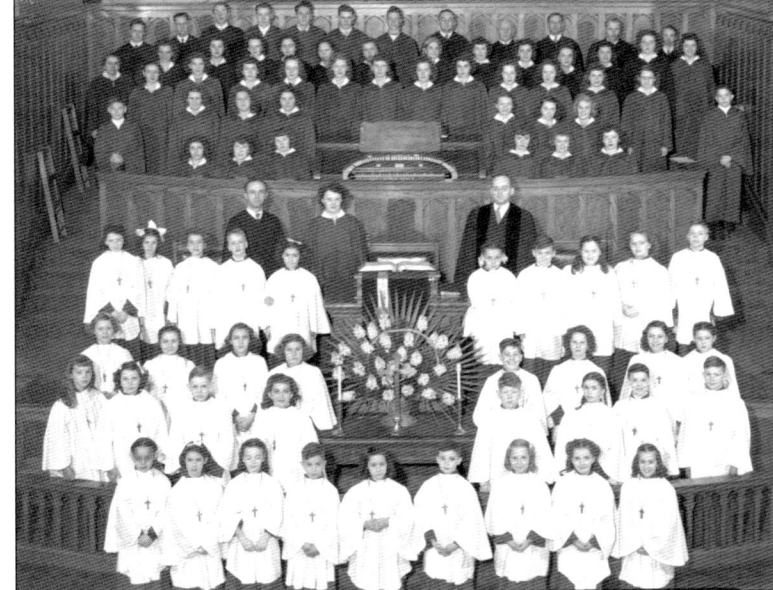

Men's group at Temple Israel, October 1947.

SOCIETY

First Presbyterian Church, Endicott, 1949.

Centenary Methodist Church on Court Street, Binghamton, June 1949.

West Presbyterian Women's Association dinner, March 7, 1950.

Ground breaking for the Holy Spirit Catholic Church, Clinton Street, Binghamton, May 7, 1950.

SOCIETY

Ethnic groups posing during the American Civic Associations "I am American" Day at the Courthouse, Binghamton, 1951.

Holy Spirit Catholic Church, Binghamton, 1952.

St. Christopher's joined Catholic churches of the area in commemorating Maundy Thursday, (the day of the Last Supper) at high mass, April 1953. Left to right: Reverend Gerald Reinmann, Reverend Vincent Kilpatrick and Reverend Robert Fehr.

SOCIETY

Beccye Fawcett, an employee of the Binghamton Public Library, works with Beccye Crawley. Fawcett was the first African-American woman hired by a library in Broome County.

Vice President Richard Nixon greets members of the Triple Cities Junior Ike Club, October 1956. The club traveled to Cornell University to meet Nixon and his wife Pat. Pictured are Marold Mastin of North High, Laraine Thuma, Gretchen Kalb and David Allen of Union-Endicott High.

Leader gives a cooking demonstration to her Girls Scouts in the 1950s.

Members of the business fund committee of Beautiful Plain Baptist Church. This committee discussed plans for an extended campaign for more than $1,000 to pay for renovations to the church located at 49 Pine Street, Binghamton, August 1955. Left to right, front: Mrs. Moses Mayo and Mrs. Leslie Fields. Back: Azalee Taylor, deacon Moses Mayo, Mrs. Calvin Wilkins, Lynn W. Woolfolk, Mrs. Lillie Colvin, Reverend George W. Brown, and George Woolfolk.

SOCIETY

First communion at Blessed Sacrament Church in Johnson City, circa 1955.
Photo courtesy Rob Donahue

Central Methodist Church, Endicott, 1957.

Reverend Richard M. Woodman, in foreground, pastor of Binghamton's First Universalist Church at 131 Front Street, September 1958.

SOUTHERN TIER MEMORIES: VOLUME II

First Baptist Church, Chenango Street, Binghamton. The church was demolished in 1970.

Girl Scouts learning how to cook, Binghamton, December 1958.

Wayne Dorsett, left, and Nancy Hunt, students of Community Baptist of Port Dickinson observe the study goals of the fourth annual school of missions being pointed out on a world map by Reverend William M. Stahl, February 1959.

SOCIETY

SS Cyril and Methodius Church before it was torn down and replaced at 150 Clinton Street, Binghamton, November 1959.

Construction of SS Cyril and Methodius Church, Binghamton, 1960.

Main Street Baptist Church, Binghamton, November 1960. (Note the children in Pilgrim outfits in front).

SOCIETY

The Rev. Thomas J. Kelleher, chaplain at St. Mary's Home, celebrated the last Mass at the home, August 1961. The nuns are from the order of Sisters of St. Joseph. The home was razed in 1962 for the construction of the $1.5 million Catholic high school in Binghamton. Father Kelleher was named chaplain at the Broome County Jail and the Broome County Home.

St. Mary's Russian Orthodox Church on Baxter Street, Binghamton, 1962.

The Windsor Civic Club dinner dance in February 1963, was planned by Susan Paquette, Mrs. William Mott and Penny Donahue, members of Girls Scout Troop 349.

Firing a salute to the late President Kennedy at the American Legion, Johnson City, November 1963.

The Reverend Richard Tomek, O.F.M. Conv., assistant pastor at St. Joseph's Catholic Church in Endicott prepares to bless palms that will be distributed during the mass on Palm Sunday. Assisting Father Tomek are altar boys, Joseph Sabol, left and Stephen Pilarcek.

Mrs. Dominic Parrotti shows off her Halloween animal, October 1964. She posed with the sculpture at her Clinton Street home.

SOCIETY

Mrs. Joseph Nosewicz, left, grand regent of the Johnson City Catholic Daughters of America, joins in conversation with Mrs. Kurt Solm, center, vice-president of religion department at Temple Israel, and Mrs. Neland Fuller, first vice-president of the Binghamton Council of United Churchwomen during the annual Interfaith Tea at Temple Israel. Some 200 women from Protestant, Catholic and Jewish faiths attended the tea in February, 1966.

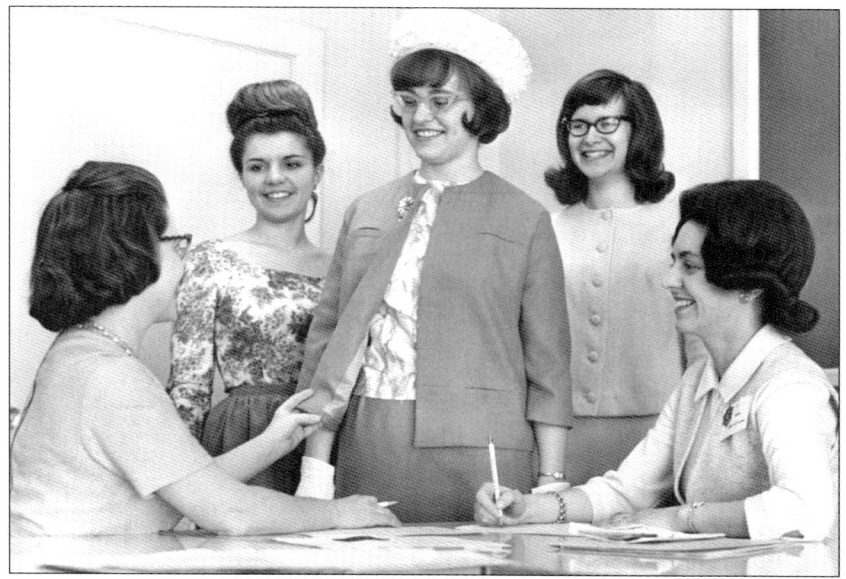

Mrs. Robert Wilson, left, and Mrs. Donald Millham, judges in a Broome 4-H annual dress review, admire fashions modeled by Sharon Ketchum, Nancy Moschak and Vickie Shapley, Binghamton, April 1965.

Mrs. Amos Main, left, hostess for the day, chats with Mrs. Robert D. Orcutt, first vice-president and chairman of the day, over a cup of tea at the Civic Club opening meeting.

Rabbi Jacob Hurwitz, spiritual leader of Temple Israel, explains religious articles of faith to nuns from three Binghamton convents, November 1966. Nuns from left: Sister M. David, a Sister of SS Cyril and Methodius, from St. Ann's Convent; Sister M. Presentia, a Felician Sister from St. Stanislaus Kostka, and Sister M. Pius, a Sister of St. Basil the Great from Holy Spirit Byzantine Convent.

SOCIETY

Mr. and Mrs. Francis V. Moran, right, show Mr. and Mrs. Taber Rich how Irishmen celebrate during the annual St. Patrick's Day semi-formal dinner dance at the Binghamton Country Club in March 1967.

Harrison E. Ludy, left, received Elk of the Year award from John E. Costello, past exalted ruler of Binghamton Lodge 852. Mr. Ludy was honored for his work as the lodge's special activities chairman, April 1967.

Mrs. Arthur Marsh, newly installed royal matron of Queen May Court 106, Order of the Amaranth, is joined by Frank Smith, left, and Merril Craft, April 1967.

The dome at St. John the Evangelist Catholic Church being re-furbished, September 1969. The church is at 1263 Vestal Avenue.

SOCIETY

Returning from the winter board of directors' meeting of the Business and Professional Women's Club of New York State held at the Biltmore Hotel in New York City. Left to right: Mrs. Louis Miller, Mrs. Letitia Holland and Mrs. James W. O'Dea.

Preparations are made for Orthodox Sunday services at the Greek Orthodox Holy Trinity Church on Court Street, Binghamton, March 1968.

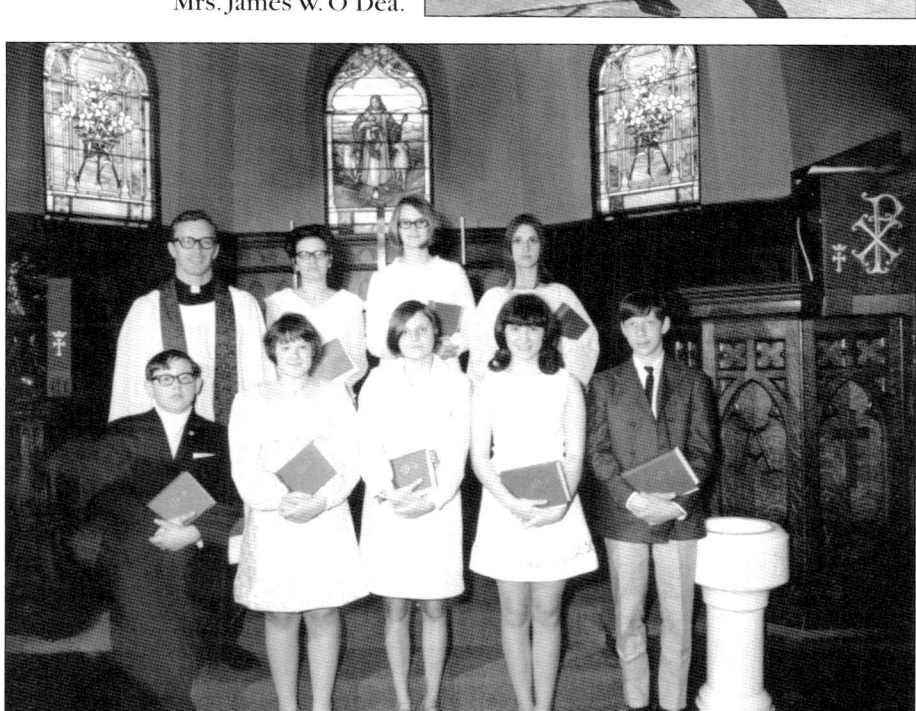

Redeemer Lutheran confirmation group, 1969.

Stephen Sadowitz, a past officer of St. John's Ukrainian Memorial Church, looks over the progress of the congregations' new structure in St. John's Parkway, July 1968.

DISASTERS

Disasters come in all types, many of them at the hands of Mother Nature. Fire, floods and windstorms can wreck buildings and kill with surprising speed.

The saddest tragedies are those inflicted by the hand of man, especially when they afflict the youngest babies.

In 1962, babies started dying at Binghamton General Hospital. The unspeakable horror was baffling at first, until authorities discovered a tragic mistake. In the room where infant formula was mixed, a can labeled "sugar" had been filled with salt. Sodium was poisoning the babies. Six died.

The community had better luck with a more traditional nemesis: flooding. Thanks to the flood-control projects built after the devastating floods of the 1930s, the Susquehanna lost much of its punch. Some areas still flooded, but the projects prevented widespread damage.

Wind and fire still packed plenty of punch, and emergency personnel scrambled to keep the community safe.

Building destroyed during the Christmas Day windstorm, 1943.

DISASTERS

A view of the damage done by the flood of 1942.

Aftermath of a Christmas Day windstorm, 1943.

Frank Brennen delivering mail in a rowboat to Walter Linden of Court Street, circa 1948. *Courtesy Carol Ann Brunell*

Roosevelt Avenue fire, Binghamton, 1957.

DISASTERS

Sanford Seed Company fire, Binghamton, 1959.

Warren Street fire, Binghamton, 1957.

Binghamton fire truck in an accident, August 1963.

An intrepid motorist plows through rising waters at the Glenwood Avenue underpass, August 1959.

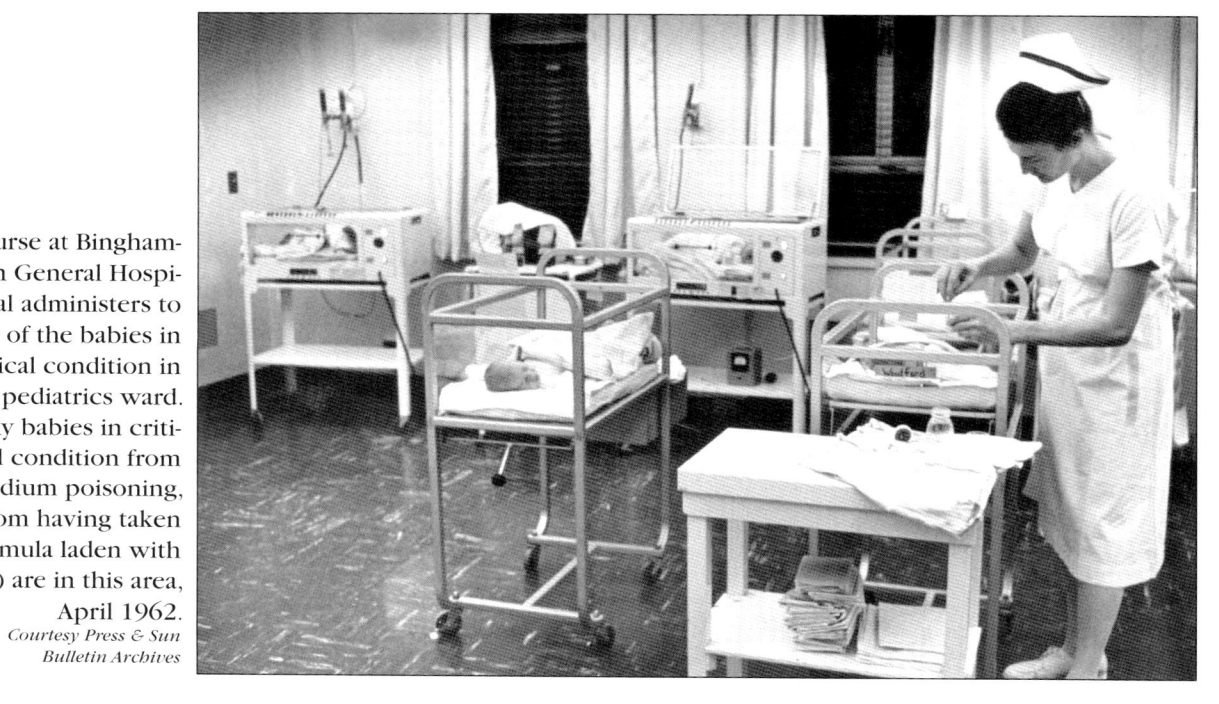

DISASTERS

A nurse at Binghamton General Hospital administers to one of the babies in critical condition in the pediatrics ward. Only babies in critical condition from sodium poisoning, (from having taken formula laden with salt) are in this area, April 1962.
Courtesy Press & Sun Bulletin Archives

City Detective John Gillen, left and Broome County District Attorney Stephen Smyk examine a can, which normally is filled with sugar, in Binghamton General Hospital's baby formula room. The can was accidently filled with salt and 6 babies died as a result, 1962.
Courtesy Press & Sun Bulletin Archives

With about 60 people listening in the hushed air of the Broome County courtroom, General Hospital Medical Director Jason K. Moyer, second from right, testifies about the babies deaths during the coroner's inquest April 1962. Flanking Dr. Moyer are: Corner Vincent M. Maddi, right, and the stenographer. Standing at left is District Attorney Stephen Smyk.
Courtesy Press & Sun Bulletin Archives

Press conference at General Hospital, 1962. Left to right, first row: John R. Normile, counsel to the Board of Managers; Patrick D. Monserrate, a law associate of Mr. Normile; Dr. F. Albert Bauman, vice-president of the hospital's medical staff, and Dr. Bruce Lott, president of medical staff. Second row: Mrs. Mary McIntyre, Mr. Normile's secretary; Stephen Smyk, District Attorney; Det. Lt. John V. Gillen; Herbert A. Kline, first assistant district attorney; Det. Capt. Michael F. O'Neil; and Camille M. Roach, second assistant district attorney. *Courtesy Press & Sun Bulletin Archives*

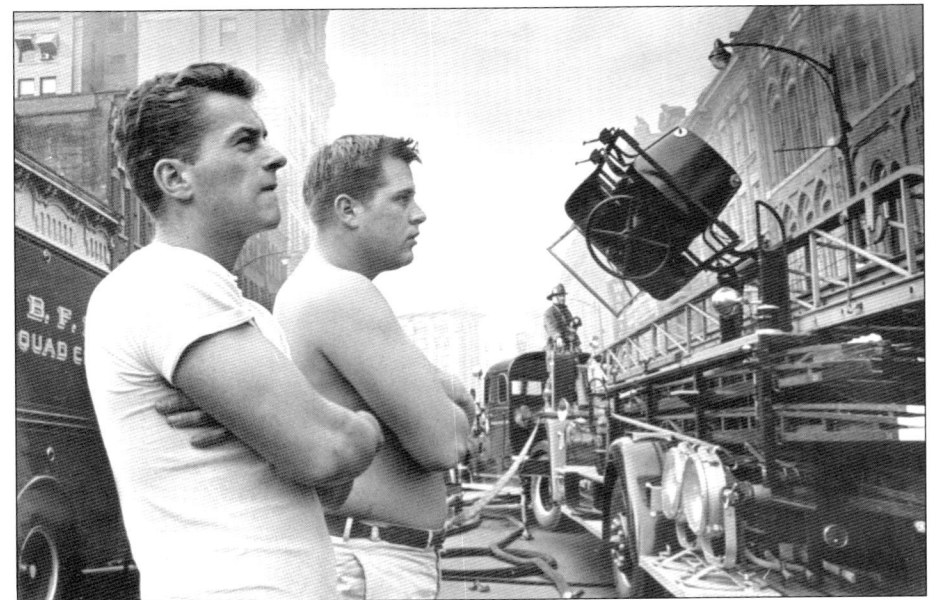

James Leonard, left and Norman Hinman, stand on Court Street, watching a fire along a half-block section in downtown Binghamton, October 1964.

Fire at the rear of the Little Venice Restaurant on Chenango Street, Binghamton, December 1964.

O.W. Sears fire on Court Street, Binghamton, 1963.

RECREATION

Baseball was king for much of the 1940s, '50s and '60s. Towns and businesses sponsored teams and the Triplets had a devoted fan base. Some of the Yankees' best players passed through Johnson Field, including Whitey Ford.

In the '60s, attendance dwindled, and the state drilled Route 17 through the old ballpark. The Yankees found a new home for their top farm club.

Regional theater groups were a passion then as they are now. Actors would do almost anything to get publicity for their shows, including climbing over tons of twisted steel.

There were dozens of companies, putting on works that have become classics such as "Harvey" and "Gentlemen Prefer Blondes."

Swimming and golf were two favorite pastimes for Broome County residents. One of the many lost benefits bestowed by the Johnson family was the pool at C. Fred Johnson Park. This mammoth swimming area was one of the largest aboveground pools in the United States.

Golf was becoming popular enough for developers to spend what was then substantial money to open new courses. Endwell Greens opened in 1967 and cost developers $300,000.

Bob Grover and the Tune Twisters, August 1947.

RECREATION

IBM Owls baseball team at Watson Field, 1940s. *Courtesy Vern Teeple*

Main Street Association Ball Club, 1941 champions. Left to right, seated: Fred Danek, Clyde "Red" Williamson, Pat Parson, Harvey Wilson and George Papastrat. Center: Howard Landon. Back row: Bob Davidson, Harry Thorpe, unidentified, Bob Steiner, Bud Felter, Dick Taylor and Bob Jacobs. Not shown: Coach Fred Danek. Sponsors: Mutual Furniture, Dickson Pharmacy, Tom Hamburon's Five and Dime Store and the A & P Store. *Courtesy Shirley Vasisko*

Farm and Home Bureau picnic at State Park, August 1947.

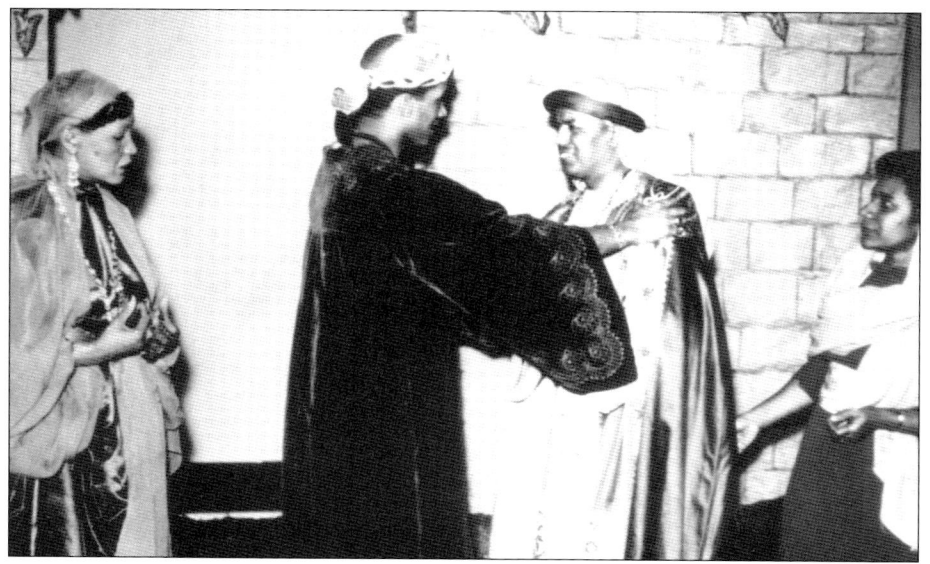

Beccye Fawcett, Allen Cave, Lloyd Sevier and Genevieve Taylor in a Christmas play.

144

Five members of the Endicott Johnson Workers Chorus help publicize a 20 year reunion, April 1964. Clockwise from banjo player George McDonald are Fowler McKune, Jack Sedlock, William Scalise and William Beddoe.

Members of the Binghamton Civic Theater rehearse "Harvey," October 1953. From left; John Kellog, Mary Halleran and Martha Humphrey.

Edward Miller gets in character as a junk dealer who becomes a millionaire overnight, October 1963. Miller starred in a production of "Born Yesterday," about a junk dealer who gets rich during World War II.

RECREATION

Golfers playing at Ely Park Golf Course, 1952.

Melody Ramblers at the WKOP studios in Binghamton, circa 1952. Left to right: Luke Corey, Irene Rice, Dick Hall and Cal Dietrich. *Courtesy Marjorie Bedford*

RECREATION

Ed "Whitey" Ford, left, was one of the many famous Yankees to pass through Broome County when the Bronx Bombers had their top farm club here.

Miller Ford President Wendell Miller poses with top winners of the Ford-sponsored Pass, Punt and Kick competition, October 1963. The winners are: Tommy Horsky, 10, Vestal; Ronnie Steenberg, 11, Binghamton; William Canny, 8, Binghamton; and Jeff Gebhart, 9, Vestal.

Two boys look at the swimming area near the Rockbottom Dam, July 1963. On shore is the old South Street Bathhouse. In the late 1960s, the city demolished the bathhouse as the swimming area fell into disuse and the river began destroying retaining walls. The key factor in the recreation area's demise was the building of the northbound segment of North Shore Drive, which virtually sealed off the area from the Seventh Ward. The boys are looking from the old Rockbottom Bridge toward the Exchange Street Bridge.

Auto racing at Five Mile Point in Kirkwood, circa 1964. Robert Page is standing at left and Gerry Heyes is standing at far right. *Courtesy Willig Vermilya*

The cast of "Gentlemen Prefer Blondes" rehearses for the Triple Cities Playhouse production, July 1953.

RECREATION

Children ride an elephant during the Port Dickinson Fire Department Circus, July 1964.

Candidates in two queen contests at the Broome County Fair meet U.S. Senator Kenneth B. Keating, July 1964. The contestants were: Nancy Waskco, Marjorie Hrath, Hope McCulloch, Barbara Worden, Willamay Zeiter, Marna Leahy, Judy Hurlburt, Kathy Resak, Marilyn Conklin, Ann York and Kay Chamberlain.

Robert Stever, president of the company that developed Endwell Greens, points across a water hazard to what will be the 16th green, September 1965. The course opened in 1967 and cost an estimated $300,000 to build.

The Susquetonics and the Question Marks stage a tug of war while joining in song, May 1964. The barbershop quartets were among units from the central and western New York region of the Society for the Preservation and Encouragement of Barbershop Quartets. The society was holding regional contests to select entries for an international competition. Pictured are: Bruce Keller, William Nash, Robert Young, Walter Stevens of the Susquetonics and Robert McColl, Paul Chaddock, George Major and Jerry Gardner of the Question Marks.

RECREATION

Johnson City Parks Superintendent H. Ray Mitchell signals "ball four" to give batter Randy Ott, a base on balls at the opening of the new season for Pony League baseball at the Village's North Side Park, June 1965. At left are Village Trustees Raymond S. Mattle, left, and Andrew J. Kavulich. At right side are Trustees Paul Silvanic, left, and Medwin A. North.

Bathers enjoy the sun and water at the CFJ Park pool, circa 1965.

Bathers enjoy the sun and water at the CFJ Park pool, circa 1965.

The Triplets could still draw large crowds when they had interesting promotions, 1966. This crowd is for Father and Son night. As with many minor league teams, attendence dwindled through the 1960s. Eventually the Triplets stadium in Johnson City was torn down to make way for Route 17 and the Yankees relocated their top farm club.

Lou Rappaport, proprietor of the House of a Thousand Items, tries to drum up support for the Triplets, April 1968. Despite the efforts of Rappaport and other community leaders, 1968 turned out to be the Triplets' last season.

RECREATION

Alice Hayes performs during the Andalucia Suite, June 1966. The Community Symphony Orchestra gave the performance at the IBM Fieldhouse.

CELEBRATION

Parades and beauty pageants seemed to be a staple of life in those innocent times. The urge to celebrate was strong, given the terrible times of the Great Depression and World War II.

The community organized a parade to honor Charles F. Johnson in 1952, one of the legendary leaders of the shoe manufacturer. Few if any marchers knew the company was a year past its employment peak.

People loved to flock to the streets with their neighbors to see what was going on. The area is traditionally Republican, and President Franklin Roosevelt was not highly regarded by most people. Amazing crowds of people flocked to see Wendell E. Wilke, the Republican businessman who lost to Roosevelt in 1940.

In that election, Wilke won Broome County in a landslide. He received 44,013 votes to Roosevelt's 30,243. The socialist candidate received 5,311.

Strong community spirit was a hallmark of those years. Hundreds of people would descend on downtown to celebrate life in Binghamton.

Owego employees of Endicott Johnson participate in a parade honoring Charles F. Johnson, 1952.

CELEBRATION

Crowd gathers on Chenango Street in Binghamton during the Christmas season.

Crowds fill the streets in Binghamton to hear Wendell L. Wilke campaign for president in 1940.

The 1940 Wendell L. Wilke campaign for president arrives in Binghamton.

Royce Allen Drum and Bugle Corps march in a parade in Binghamton, circa 1940.
Courtesy Sylvia Follette

Group assembled for a parade honoring the Veterans of Foreign Wars, at 65 Carroll Street, Binghamton, November, 1947.

United Defense Fund entry in a September 1952 parade in Binghamton.

Susquehanna Valley Home float during a parade in Binghamton, September 1952.

Daniel R. Stainbrook, chairman of the Miss Broome County Scholarship Pageant Committee, discusses qualifications and responsibilities for entering the Miss Broome County Pageant, a preliminary to the 1969 Miss America Pageant, sponsored by the Endicott Junior Chamber of Commerce. From left: Miss Judith Randall, Miss Antoinette Lambrinos, Miss Delores Buza, Miss Kathleen Grose and Miss Diane Brown.

CELEBRATION

Endicott Police Captain William J. Norton, shines up the shoes of Patrolman Richard Andrascki in preparation for the annual Endicott-Vestal Policemen's Ball, December 1960.

Lieutenant Governor Frank C. Moore chats with Miss Muriel Turk, left, "Miss Broome County," and Mrs. Shirley Tryon, "Miss Sixty," after the two queens of the Johnson City 60th anniversary celebration were crowned at Johnson Field, July 1952.

Charles F. Johnson, Jr., studies plans for Endicott Johnson's 50th anniversary celebration, August 21-26, 1956. Seated, left to right: Mrs. Theodora Kneebis and Mr. Johnson. Standing: Alexander Koval, Stanley Stephens and Michael Scelsi.

Youthful members of the Conklin Castlemen Junior Drum and Bugle Corps form a color guard at a Veterans Day Parade, November 1964. The corps was sponsored by the Conklin American Legion Post 1845.

CELEBRATION

Crowds celebrate Binghamton's centennial as a city, 1967. Binghamton was incorporated as a village in 1834. The first New Englanders moved to the region about 1790.